Sonnets
In Perilous Times

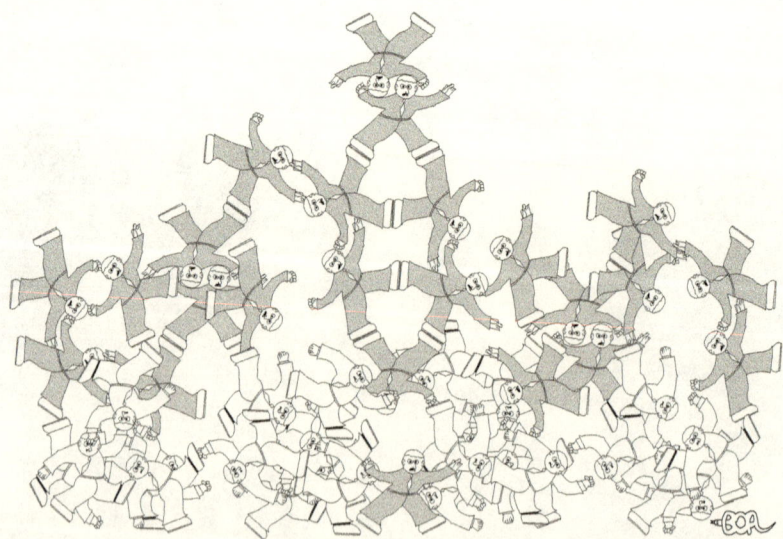

Sonnets
In Perilous Times

Bruce Adam

ᔰᕈ Ara Pacis ᕈᔰ

Ara Pacis Publishers
Des Plaines, IL 60016
www.arapacispublishers.com

ISBN-10: 1-938902-15-7
ISBN-13: 978-1-938902-15-4

Library of Congress Control Number: 2019915227
Manufactured in the United States of America.

Contents

Perilous Times

Paul's letter to Timothy made it plain,
That perilous times would come in last days;
Later, a group of more than forty vain
Zealots would hatch a plot against Paul's ways
Swore not to eat or drink a thing at all
Until they'd seen to it that he was dead.
The days crawled by as they watched their plan stall:
Forty-plus empty guts yearned to be fed;
Minds grown fully charged with resolution
To forget Paul, to eat and drink again
Went their separate ways in dissolution,
Their demise now linked to the first days when
True strength forms in spirit, through the divine,
Not from milk and honey, but bread and wine.

Introduction

In his essay *Religion and Literature*, T.S. Eliot wrote, *Literary criticism should be completed by criticism from a definite ethical and theological standpoint.* When I began my studies, religion and tradition were not in doubt. When I really came to understand the use of the term *Tradition*, it opened a way to comprehend poets by the *traditional* character of their contribution. Those readers who understand and accept tradition, as Eliot explained it in his essay, *Tradition and the Individual Talent*, will know what I mean, where each new writer slightly alters the existing order in the present, directed by the past. There is something deeply philosophical about this, but I think one has to love poetry to really care and see how it matters. The notion that poetry could influence the world, not just in a subtle way but profoundly, harkens back to Shelley's definition of the poet being an *unacknowledged legislator*. It's not difficult to catch this meaning, but it also carries a kind of emphasis on the fact that there is something pathetic or impotent going on like Cassandra having the power of prophesy but the accompanying curse that nobody would believe her. Nietzsche alluded to a similar idea in *Thus Spake Zarathustra* when he wrote of the world revolving invisibly around great ideas born far from the marketplace.

So it isn't very likely, is it, that poetry would be considered a viable or essential weapon in confronting a world where ideology changes laws to no longer be spiritually compatible with the thought of *poetic and philosophical legislators?* On the other hand, it would have to be said at some point that those who think clearly, who understand real poetry and hold its principles at heart, would detect when the world had gone off the proper course, so to speak.

But by leaps and bounds the world is far off course, much as if the keepers of the flame themselves substituted burned-out torches for what gives off true light, as if expecting us to say, *Don't think twice, it's alright.* Thus it occurred to me to create this volume of sonnets in the hope that it would provide a way to think about some of these changes, not just to literature generally but to the free world specifically, and the dangers of continuing on this path. Sadly, it feels like building a temple in an encroaching jungle, knowing it will be lost but finishing it anyway in the hope that someday it will be found.

On the other hand, it's war. Sonnets are often thought of as being love poems, and one would not think they would be the first choice for an artist to address a spiritual crisis, but it started to make sense to me. The *French Resistance* used the most innocuous objects to camouflage the transportation of weapons to use in their fight against Hitler. They would take huge risks to deliver flowers that concealed guns, knowing that daily life must go on, and not every cart would be checked. A sonnet, like a loaf of bread, can hold a lot gun powder.

Directions

These poems may look peaceful, but they're grenades,
Handle with care, and they will activate
Until you'll hold power that never fades,
But do it soon, for there's no time to wait.
This is not a drill but a call to war;
Armed with the truth on this great battlefield,
Become a weapon no one can ignore
On target from firm ground that will not yield;
You just have to open up to receive
The full charge, and then your shell will let go.
These bombs are smart, so real they make believe
The hard cases who deny what they know
Conscience acknowledges, whose will to fight
The truth comes from darkness that hates the light.

Years ago, my late friend Ford Russell wrote me that he was considering as a doctoral thesis the idea that Tennyson's *In Memoriam* was an attempted synthesis of Christian and Classical values, that its form and structure are a uniting of various genres associated with the Christian and Classical traditions. The poem's method, for example, grew out of a tradition started by Coleridge of devotional literature prominent in the Broad Church Movement. There is something like that going on in this book of sonnets: an urgent attempt to clear the bramble from the path so that a true examination of what it means to be alive can again take place. I believe that any truly honest approach to life leads to a *cross roads*, literally to the question of immortality of the soul, and living in this world is always going to present a dichotomy or tension between the inner life and the world outside, where one attempts to unite the two, which have not been tending to mix very well lately to say the least. In the best of times, one is generally free to do this without a sense of danger or dark clouds descending. Many of these poems concern the conscious reaction to there being a suppression not only of religious truth but the right to attempt to think well through the same questions that every honest individual will face. There is a need for rebellion against the current climate and culture of political correctness, absolutist in its attempts to block off anyone searching for the absolute. In *The Rebel*, Albert Camus wrote, *How would society define an absolute? Perhaps everyone is looking for this absolute on behalf of all. But society and politics only have the responsibility of arranging everyone's affairs so that each will have the leisure and the freedom to pursue this common search.* Literature exists as part of our search for the absolute, which is due to the natural desire *to find peace through a satisfaction of the whole being,* to borrow a phrase from T.S. Eliot's preface to Pascal's *Pensées,* and it was Pascal who said in Pensée 347 *All our dignity consists...in thought. By it we must elevate ourselves, and not by space and time which we cannot fill. Let us endeavour, then, to think well; this is the principle of morality.* The more that freedoms are curtailed and thought is controlled, the deeper underground traditional literature and clear thinking will go to make it safe to come out again.

Goethe said, *Theory fits life like the human body fits the cross,* so theory will die off because while it might seem to fit our shape, its only goal is to shape us by force, and it is in our nature to rebel for our right to be free. Truth, on the other hand, makes life thrive, growing up like a vine and giving life deeper roots. Though history appears to be a long roller coaster where corruption seems eventually to be overturned, we need not let ourselves be taken for such a ride. Rather we must now put this fight at the center of our lives. We need to deconstruct political correctness and defend our right to search for truth even with our lives. When truth is suppressed and in short supply, perilous times unfold, one sign being when people of faith come under increasing attack from those without faith; like now, for example, and it shouldn't be surprising that sonnets like these would appear in defense of tradition and its values in what are also *prayerless times.*

~ Bruce Adam
September 21, 2019

*Truth is so obscure in these times, and falsehood so established,
that unless we love the truth, we cannot know it.*

~ Pascal

Sonnets
In Perilous Times

To Thomas Sanfilip
A deep soul and resonant voice

And in memory of Armelle Desplanches
A patient teacher, free spirit, and
insatiable, curious reader who loved
and embraced literature of the highest order

Inanimate Objections

Let the whole world of things each have a mind
So bikes won't let you ride them, and the door
Not let you in, nor coffee let you grind,
Unless they approve of what you stand for.
When your beliefs all properly conform
To standards required for personal views
Your umbrella will open in a storm
Your car will start, and the fridge won't refuse
To open. You'll be able to shower,
Your bed will wave you through and let you sleep,
But you must acknowledge what has power
Or you won't buy or sell, nor sow and reap.
When clothes won't let you wear them, you will see
That you'll never fit if you disagree

The Rock

We encounter the rock, not as a group —
But somewhere in the past, some one of us,
an ancestor with much strength and great heart,
came upon it and noted its presence,
described its dimensions and guessed its weight.
The sheer force of it took shape in his words,
and the words became the rock as he moved
beyond it and left it there where it stood.
Everyone now seems to question those words
that some now dispute the rock itself, doubt
whether it exists or was encountered
in the first place. So now there's a new search,
except this time seekers must close their eyes,
and feel for it, hands tied behind their backs.

Lot in our Day

Lot in our day would have led his people out
of Sodom, warning them to not look back,
and arrived with all intact after the march;
But months later there would be symptoms
going around as those who peeked began
a gradual change into pillars of salt.
For some, it would happen within the year;
They would be those who took the longest look,
even wished to go back except it was on fire.
Others, who may have only peeked slightly,
would be transformed within five years or so.
Some would last ten: those who only squinted
an instant; the rest of natural causes
but opened up found to be sacks of salt.

Jolly Roger

Fully adult, unable to choose good,
Unwilling to call the diversions sin
The whole idea of doing as one should
Lost in the swelling incidental bin
Of salted-down experience, the ship
So long at sea, a scurvy sets in. Piles
In the hold let go and slide in each dip,
Wave upon wave compiling what defiles
Sickened, diseased, what used to be a soul
Lost at sea, no compass, no steering wheel
No North Star above to guide toward a goal
In fog and doldrums, hauled along the keel
And in the crow's nest, none to yell, *Land ho!*
... No one's jolly indentured to the foe

Refutation of the Left

I am a refutation of the left
And prove it all false to its very core
By my spirit's life. It's not just bereft,
But empty of everything and then more:
It's at absolute bottom of the chain
Of being, tries to drag your spirit down,
Does all it can to make sane look insane
And make you both a criminal and clown.
But inside I can laugh at this dead weight
And how far into the murk it has sunk
Because in the end I can see its fate
In the history of failed utter bunk.
But in the meantime keep a watchful eye
As they want those who refute them to die.

Wreckage

Because they all showed up and were all strange,
Wanting not to be normal but change the view,
Force the world to completely flip the range,
And dismiss each traditional value,
The news spread of their sordid affair
Where sordid was redefined, relative
And flattened into *Everything is fair,*
Nothing is wrong, just go live and let live.
But though it's taught in church not to judge
And to love God and neighbors as ourselves,
Faith was put on trial, while they wouldn't budge,
Wanting books about them in schools on shelves.
All this from the politically correct
Which cares not, won't see, the world it has wrecked

Homestead

My homestead has become a vast open
land of lush forests that meet the desert
in a clash of great rock formations and
badlands surging with geological
wonders, geysers, waterfalls and the like
There are lakes beyond belief, salt and fresh,
a great mountain range with rivers winding
all through it, each its own ecosystem.
And all of this in what, ten or so rooms,
a shed in the backyard and a garage?
But somehow it has gotten so massive
that I can't find anything in the sprawl
and when my mind connections fail, they will
turn into wilderness with my last breath

Out in the Open

Evil doesn't have to hide anymore
It's out in the open, plain as can be
Makes a huge mainstream push we can't ignore
Sees who's not on board and notices me
I try to keep my profile very low
When evil speaks, it spins it all to seem
The good are evil, the evil good, so
Those still in the middle, living a dream
Join up thinking they're doing something good
Buy into lies, which turns to opting out
Of truth, ignorant that it's all falsehood,
Which deceives so well those fooled have no doubt.
Therefore the words, *They know not what they do*
And, *Events are in the saddle...* ring true

Life at the Wall

We reached the wall and saw jugglers. They kept
Ideas going in symmetric display
So compelling big-hearted men have wept
At what's called proof the mind's the only way.
The wall's a great backdrop for such a crowd,
Both performers and those who come to learn
If anything might be behind the shroud,
At which the nay-sayers do a slow burn
At the suggestion the wall's not an end.
They demand letting acrobats distract
And declare that prayers and wailing offend;
That hitting the wall means just facing fact.
None of this proves anything, it's just how
Life looks at the wall if you go there now.

Above the Fray

The beach tells the ocean, *Cease and desist*
The going back and forth that leaves the sand
Covered, then exposed; angry as with fist
Raised: There is force in the beach's demand.
The sea senses a more powerful force
In and out of itself breathing these tides,
Respiring as it were, as the true source
Of these effects, feels something real that hides
Somehow, at least from the jagged shoreline,
Which for the impact blames only the sea.
Ponds and streams don't slosh this way, and lack brine,
So to the beaches, what else could it be?
Meanwhile the moon, part of a larger whole,
Stays above conflicts between reason and soul.

A Choosing Place

In a short phrase, this world's a choosing place
You decide which way you will go, to good
Or to evil; you cannot form a base
Between them. For you would be made of wood,
Unable to think, quite dead to the choice
But this is just what many are. They do
Not live to stand for something, have no voice
To pierce through the shadowy middle zoo
Where beings basically mill in a herd
Driven by media, told what to think
A rational idea would be absurd
From what could be termed a collective stink
Meanwhile those who choose the good come to terms
With the nature of earth, crawling with worms

Fugitive Thoughts

Sometimes unexpectedly, fugitive
thoughts arrive as if out of the jungle
telling tales so compelling, familiar
though in amazing fragments that carry
a full share of the whole like a fracture
of a hologram, that somehow it all
makes sense, connects, rivets our attention
for a moment to review as a dream,
for anything bearing on what it means
for ourselves, we are so desperate
for any news that comes from the unseen,
which somehow we know soon as we hear it.
We live on the edge of this wilderness,
one of our purposes to listen in.

Signal Wire

Whatever is the message of this time,
I receive nothing. Ransacking my brain,
I repeat, turns up nothing to report.
But I'm infused like a wire with signals
even if I'm no demodulator,
no radio, certainly no beacon,
just a man at his desk with a pencil
awaiting further orders, burning with
Saint Elmo's fire, almost invisible,
glowing so slightly that it can't be seen
except when there's an absolute darkness,
as when there's a convergence of bad news,
a gathering of forces of evil
where we all broadcast the recessive light

Babylon All Over

When I succumb at last as all men must
And this whole generation's gone away
And all new eyes regard us not as dust
But for all we did; what we had to say
I'm sorry we won't be there to be shamed
Not for Babel built so high that it fell
Nor for Sodom and Gomorrah, untamed
Immoral cities that transferred to hell
We did our share, changed laws given by God
Some didn't like it that six thousand years
Of wisdom and good example felt odd
So out they went, while we clinked a few beers.
If we took what we've done back on time trips
All other eras would chase us with whips

Aura

I saw her on a pamphlet in a dream,
More like a video phone, where she said
I had a cogent aura, a faint gleam
And she couldn't get it out of her head.
I knew what she meant, as I'd felt it too
Coming from her, not imagined inside.
I told her there was nothing one could do,
That it's not like you're able to decide
To have this glow: you do or you do not.
At that, the connection broke, and later,
The aura left me. Dark, empty, it got
Worse as I kept trying to locate her.
The pamphlet was no longer like a phone:
Just a pamphlet about being alone.

Weight of the World

People walking around wearing stocks
Saying *How you doing? I'm doing fine,*
This one for making a revealing tweet
That one self inflicted, slow suicide
For knowing that he's wrong but cannot change
Repentance by itself, with will to sin.
To pray and then go on the internet
To the dark web and enjoy wearing chains
And having no hope, just letting all go,
It's a tragic intuition, so much
Pain just masked, concealed by huge appetite
For pleasure, which offsets it to a degree.
The weight of the world is upon us all:
The ball and chain we drag despite the key.

Bookshelves

The books are all pressed so tight on the shelves
That I have a rough time pulling one out
And give up on poets and others
Sitting down instead to write down these words
There was a time when I thought the poets
Not so much all drank out of the same stream
As they all had in their heads the same gleam
One book of life, and all on the same page
But I've moved on out of that wooded glen
To acknowledging the meanderings
Of spirit mind, some leading while misled
All wrapped up in the knitted veil, the truth
Seen through their eyes. One still must think well to
Discern vague sparks where darknesses collide

Paper Owl

I see it in a cemetery tree
High up on a limb in the early spring,
Paper shaped like an owl, weathered, where we
Would think it's alive, so real is the wing,
The ears, and the dignity of the perch
That all says, here is the bird we call wise;
And to my surprise on a closer search
I see printed words the world has called lies:
The ones known to be real when in the heart
Where they come alive, awaken the soul
To know there's more than what we know in part,
That incomplete and doomed, we'll be made whole,
Says the paper owl with Revelation
Atop a tree in our devastation.

11

Around the Sun

The world is being taken for a ride,
under one cup, then another, a bean
lost in a shell game, tucked in palm or sleeve.
The world looks on, wondering where it went,
fooled into believing it's here or there
while the cup's always empty everywhere.
The game is run by shysters, shameless slugs,
who rely on the trust of good ol' folks,
who do not see their pockets being picked
who do not know the playing field is sloped.
The tortured spinning wheel goes round and round
and where she stops, the world is lost, not found.
It lands on hatred...fear...greed...lust — and spins
on and on, under this cup...no, that one!

Meeting at Armageddon

There's no happy ending, just a long fight
With evil that won't change, so it must die;
So we meet at Armageddon tonight
No mercy. Annihilation's our cry.
Because they claim to have God on their side,
We've chosen to let Satan's banner fly
Let none survive, and God will be denied,
Their funeral pyre will ignite the sky.
So this will be the end, the final clash
That proves we have power to beat God's plan;
The last thing they will see is our teeth gnash,
Their last thought will be the glory of man;
Then we'll all be free at last to be first,
Nothing to stop our quenching any thirst.

New Orthodoxy

I asked the scientist, *Is there a God?*
No, there's nothing out there in all of that,
He replied, *but there's still room to be awed.*
Are we alone? I asked, smelling a rat.
No, how could there not be something out there
In all of that? he answered, looking up
And sweeping his arm full across the air.
We're random, so, there's much more in the cup.
Then he ran some experiments to show
How life forms, short of making life himself,
And when it failed I asked how one could know.
He put everything back up on the shelf
You lack all faith, he said, *for not seeing,*
Blessed are the rest just for agreeing.

To the Doctor Leaving the Aborted Child
To Die "In Comfort" on the Table

Are there any words as the seconds tick?
Are you wiping smudges from the brushed steel?
Do you make a call, check someone who's sick
To feel like a doctor, ignore what's real?
This is full term, so it will take a while
There will be crying, which you must ignore.
Perhaps with headphones and a playlist file
You can do paperwork to dull the roar.
On busy days, this maternity ward
Motherless, yet softened with pastel tones,
Between the operating room and morgue
Is a place of life, rest for tiny bones.
Is there a wall for pictures of each face?
How do you scrub your wall of such disgrace?

13

All Our Hands in This
After Shelley

I met a recluse here in my home town
who told me: A fountain of spirit springs
in a garden. All around, from above
and within, a kind and loving spirit
watches over, bringing wonder of what
it could be, composed of nothing but love.
And if you were to speak to the spirit
and engage it, you would be filled with truth,
where all questions would be answered at once.
But suddenly there is a disturbance:
the law broken where the spirit, closing
the garden, says, *All have a hand in this.*
Signs remain: Its truth still wells up, making
gardens out of stone-cold hearts, desert wrecks.

Resonator

If I can write one truth, one simple truth
That has yet to have been isolated,
I think it would remind me
Of a simple petroglyph on a cliff
Left thousands of years ago
By a man trying to communicate
To the ages of something like the hunt
Trees on the cliff blow on a windy day,
Their leaves rustling in a strange way, almost
As if they were tied to the petroglyphs
And the simple truth is that I feel it —
I sense the interaction, the spirit
Not just in the carving but in nature
With me — a resonating instrument

Heart of Tufa Stone

I've lived so long I have an underground —
Tunnels and catacombs throughout my soul
My thoughts echo when I sit in silence
Resounding in these deep inner caverns
It is a kind of hollow, rushing noise
As if what was once a river trickles
With that familiar drip in a bucket
Not the mighty crash of deep inner waves
There's also the lure of old memories
That sing like sirens calling out to me
Yes, it's true. I let them tear me apart
Then crawled back to my husk, a broken soul —
Before worms will have me, my own had me
Leaving a jagged but resonant maze

Geometry

The nature of any one man's the map
For the makeup of the world in its sin.
Man is a fractal, his geometry
Has the same look with one or with millions,
The landscape of his soul is much the same
As what we would see writ large in the world.
The same basic faults in society
Interlace the heart of one man the same;
The same basic stresses and tendencies
Whether to anger, greed or no concern,
Lurk in the same proportions in one man
Or the village, the city where he lives;
Even a war can be seen in one life,
Burned-out cities found in a heart besieged.

Concerto of the Dead

It's a limited existence, the stream
Picks you up, then gives you the shortest ride
And drops you off, perchance, you think, to dream,
But somewhere along the line you decide
What it means to you, how you'll play along;
Going with the flow or against the grain
Exuding an outlook into a song
That gets others humming in the same vein,
An army of voices throbbing one will,
Put to the test on a great battlefield,
You safely watch what unfolds from a hill.
All bow to you for never having kneeled:
Soon enough, time's train blows a far-off horn:
Concerto of the dead for the unborn.

Dry Heave

I said there might be something to scrape off
something important deep inside my soul
And she just laughed at me, with some concern
that I took myself so seriously
But so much had been pouring out of me
for days and days, now I was down to dregs,
but in those I felt there could be something,
something quite meaty, something very big
It all goes to a sense it must be there
How could it not be? After all, human
as I am, hell bent on wringing myself
like a wet rag, there must be something there
But no matter how hard I push or heave
I come up empty though I still believe

More Past than Present

You're more past than present now and will fade
But a bee sting can keep tingling for days
Its presence is short, but memory long
And causes one's view of flowers to change
Knowing *whodunnit*, you don't look for clues
Instead advance to the courtroom, and there
Apply truth and justice, God's will be done
Since you can't bring life back to anyone
The same goes for love, just to clear the air
I more than adored you, unseen new hues
Colored our spirits, wavelengths of wide range
Connected hearts and minds in bonds thought strong
Until you stabbed me for trusting God's ways
And all I think now is, *What a dull blade!*

Spear of Truth

One day a spear of truth went through my brain
And pinned me on a tree where I can't move
Just like a note on a bulletin board
That some might see as they walk by and read
The spear was one of true revelation
Which I wouldn't leave even if I could
Being what it is, such truth leaves no choice
And so I became its servant, pinned there.
Now in this posture, if that defines it,
I have messages, all born of the spear
Which are shot out like darts to those passing
Some close their eyes, denying I am there
And dodge them, while other focus their sight
To let it hit them right between the eyes.

Essence of Faulkner

I'm never going to stop saying this
Evil is easier to make than good
We know it better — it's more compelling —
We're better at destroying than building
At criticizing than complimenting
At hating over loving everyone
We're good at taking the easy way out
Great at breaking the very laws we make
Especially the first ten made for us
Which we cannot deny make total sense
On even the most cursory study —
But it's the mind that's the enemy
The heart is the source for all that is good
Where we wish to be better than we are

The Beast

Conditions in a world that lost its minds
No longer here actually to engage
Dead and unable to participate
A legion of honorable souls
Who in their own time had a great impact
And even now exert some influence
Though it's gradually diminishing
Concentrated into one large bookshelf
That can easily be dismissed or banned
Without one word of objection from them
A world without great minds is a sad time
There's a sense of emptiness and chaos
As liars and bullies vie for power
Then the beast cracks the egg and emerges

Planned Parenthood

Mengele wished to do experiments
And his tools were quite crude by our standards
Nothing we have today will do better
Given lines that must be crossed to proceed
Our character as people of the earth
Must be established not just by standards
Written into law but based in the heart.
What is less obscene, using aborted
Children as a source to experiment
Or Jews the Nazis believed subhuman?
Such thinking turns around the other way
Making subhuman the supposed thinker
These are crimes of reason — to ignore them
Is to pave a road straight to a death camp

Something Real

They all have nice names, but yours has my mind
They're all beyond reach, but I reach for you
They all have their quirks, and though yours are worst
I don't give them a thought, but you the works
It's like I'm on a hunt but cannot find
The place where the hunt's taking place, it's true
You always needled me, and when I'd burst
You'd pout until I caved, the king of jerks
Somehow, in the great pond, there's just one swirl,
A whirlpool or a drain that I can't plug
It all boils down that there is just one girl
Who makes me feel a monarch and a bug
So in the fakery there's something real
And only you (God knows why) makes me feel

19

Unformed in Formation

Tasked with bringing the unformed up to speed
The informed come to find out they are banned
The unformed have decided in their greed
To take control, which is their first demand
They claim to be already informed, so
They're telling off professors of each class
Claiming teachers are uninformed and slow.
Youth's energy's equal to Times Square's mass,
Sign here. The faculty lines up to sign
Why not? They've learned they're equal, so they should
Make up new rules at the speed of light. Fine,
But please don't come to my door (knock on wood).
Students shall be fathers to the teachers
As new gods form to inform old preachers

Strong Good Stone

When the time comes for you to choose your rock
You have a vast choice and know your own taste
I am amazed by the variety
It is easy to see how tastes differ —
Some choose sedimentary while others
Prefer something metamorphic
Or igneous — As for myself, I like
Petrified wood with some chatoyancy
So that's the rock I'll choose to block others
Now I have it placed in front of my house
So when you walk by you can enjoy it
Along with those my neighbors selected
Walking our streets will give you examples
Of strong good stone for making good strong walls

What is Real

They ask what's real, put a thought in your mind
that nothing is, that there's no meaning here —
say a rock is solid, but what we find
is energy toward mass. But what of fear?
Isn't that real enough? What's it made of?
Being contradicts laws that lessen life,
reduce it to enzymes, pools without love...
Then lightning strikes, and soon one has a knife
and other tools, out hunting to survive —
until there's suddenly you, here and now
in this day and age, working hard to thrive,
with who, what, when where; without why or how;
— which works until you find love: Then what's real
is how and why streaming through all you feel.

Music of the Spheres

There's music on the far side of the moon,
Volcanic eruptions on Io, too;
As when I leave your planet pull, I'm soon
A flameless pit, empty orchestra hall,
An ashen landscape without fiery soul,
No music giving life to the place; ball
Of no direction, sphere of little use.
But when in tandem with my proper you,
The timeless laws of physics draw me whole,
Complete as what I'm made to be: not loose,
But secured freely where my heart belongs.
Then our engines start as powerful fields
Take hold, sustaining molten cores, in songs
That transform night to auras to our shields

21

You Make Your Own Demons

You make your own demons, and the devil
Shows you how, gives you all the tools you need
With blueprints, and takes over while you sleep;
Helps to finish the job in vivid dreams
So when you wake each waking day, the web
Has one more strand, one new bar in the jail,
The cell that contains and eats you alive.
But before you're done, you can still revel
Unaware that the deadly planted seed
Like kudzu will kill all you hoped to reap
Where the lush green field is not what it seems
The sea grows so sick as algae blooms ebb
And flow, so thick one can no longer sail,
It's a wonder truth's able to survive

Twister

On a trail back home I rediscover
A twister, the revolving face of death.
As I stand here, I know I still love her
As it whirls and roars, I can feel her breath —
I remember the day we built a tent
Here in these same mountains, in pouring rain,
filled with such passion, it was heaven sent...
Water streamed around us. It was insane
that night — so many frogs on a back road
we left a dead-frog tire trail for some miles.
There was clearly a deep fantastic code
in it, cogent symbols swirled to our smiles
A centered eye our spirits surged in;
Natives of the scar wind stirs as surgeon.

Why We're Blind

Let's plead a wider case of why we're blind
Which will do more I think to help us see
Than having anger that the world won't change
You don't see me better than I see you
You want to be seen as you are, that's clear
And if we'd start from there, if you would look
As carefully as you wish to be seen
Make *thinking clearly* the goal, it would mean
You'd begin to read the world like a book,
And distinguish what the truth is from fear
Which would have impact on all that you do
Where injustice and ignorance are strange
Because knowledge and truth are there for free
But in the end are too often declined

Assumptions

Don't assume political ideas true;
The big lies engulf but can't pass a test
Of simple logic, at which they recoil
And show their claws and fangs to shut you down
They oppose hate, so why do they impose
Hate so freely and dismiss all backlash?
Do as I say, not as I do, the joke
Works as sought ends trump what's true; it's just smoke
And so it's ok to loot in a clash
That starts up with lies that everyone knows
Not because someone's skin is black or brown
Though that makes the snake begin to uncoil,
Justifies striking, saying it's oppressed,
Tells lies in spades then sneaks in for the coup.

A Hundred Days From You

A hundred days out, the ship hit a reef
And stranded me a hundred days from you
Now we're on another boat, going home
And you host parties all night with old friends
While I stand at the rail watching the moon
I both dread and long now to see the dock
So I can disembark and start my life
But you keep popping up like an old wife
With the key to my heart that has no lock
I see no land, so we won't get there soon
Feel like you surfaced too fast, but the bends
Have me, and you dance barefoot in the foam
Frothing from my mouth. Washed up, I come to...
The truth pounds over. My pulse will be brief.

Blowback

There isn't anything that one can say
Without a strident reaction by some
Anymore than ships docked along the bay
Can avoid barnacles. So it is dumb
To worry or listen to all voices
When they'll be shouting all across the board
Take the opposite view among choices
And the same will happen. To be ignored
Say and do nothing, which is the first rule
Of the unknown citizen as it were
But not the attitude one learns in school
Which should teach how to prevail and endure
I expect to soon be under attack
So I've scraped and rigged to sail in blowback

The Window is My Mother

The window is my mother. I was born
Through a pane on one side, one of the eyes;
You can see the face, with curtains all torn
By tears she shed once but no longer cries
I sense her in the darkness, through soft light,
A subtle emanation from the moon;
She died some years ago, I cried that night
But stopped the tears by the next afternoon
Wiping my eyes first, then the windows clean
Parting the curtains that had veiled her view;
That made her choose wrong from right, made her mean;
It started when her father's window blew
Open a full Pandora's box, where hope,
The one good thing, left when it couldn't cope

Prescription

Just give it to me straight, Doc, what's the truth?
Labyrinthine wonders in wet caverns
Beyond reach somewhere west of River Styx
Begin to think you see them in taverns
Made to leave alone since we'd take our picks:
A geode cracked open, air would destroy
Sights to behold in mind, not to be held
An extra buck in a carnival booth
Gives a glimpse, tattooed lady for a boy
No hope to dream it without a mind meld
It's a rip-off, a promise you won't die
Then sucks life out of you, no reason why
You're better off not asking. Don't go deep.
What was that you said, Doc? I fell asleep.

Stalking the Chaff

What happens when you let bad ideas pass
For the real truth when they lack what it takes?
I don't know. I'm a tall blade of green grass
And I know nothing at all about fakes.
What happens when you let lie after lie
Compound, but ignore that, sell them as true?
I don't know, I'm just a ripe stalk of rye
Waiting to be threshed by someone like you.
And what happens when you let evil rule
And turn blind eye to injustice and hate?
I'm not sure, but I'm not the one who is cruel;
I have enough to deal with on my own plate.
What will you say when the fields are all plowed?
I don't know, but I sure won't say it loud.

The Pathetic Night

Love is like light, to draw it's not the same
Light blue paint depicting sky is not sky
So too, how do you love without a name?
We talk of truth in what is all a lie.
This is a liar's playground, some big game.
It's all appearances. Behind each veil
Though, there are computer screens, all the same
And each one spinning out in great detail
One avatar or more, each with a name
But more like masks at a masquerade ball
It all comes down to how one plays the game
You don't deal with true others but their doll
But in this darkness, people still crave light
So love's most faked in the pathetic night

A Trust in Order

I'm just going to fall and die it's true,
Somewhere some unknown time, life hits the fan,
But when I go down, I'll be brave for you;
Because of you, I'll take it like a man
Without you in my life, I had no ground
I floated lost, an untethered balloon
Fearing new directions, I was bound
To whims of the winds like an earthless moon
Now I have all I need in a home base
Whole in synchronous orbit with the spheres;
I sometimes feel I'm flying held in place
And hardly notice the passing of years
A kind of trust in order has evolved
Where any fears I had have been resolved

Stuck Veil

Let's play *wear veils* and hope to take them off
But when the time comes move to where it's dark
Let others do it. We're here to scoff,
To role play, to witness others go stark
Raving mad, and then be mad at the trolls
Who drove them to it but be glad they're there
For the entertainment. We've sold our souls
But deny it to one another; fair-
Minded are we, though quite blind to the core
We take from this world what we want. Who cares
Who gets hurt? If no one does, it's a bore
And on the screen, these really aren't affairs.
That's why we wear the veils. Mine's on for good:
Evil lets no one look under the hood.

Clarification

The laughing matter does not in itself
Project darkness — It is not itself dark
When we say, *That is no laughing matter,*
Darkness is exposed to leave laughter out
But imagine there's a laughing matter —
But we are called to abandon darkness
And laugh freely, fully at its expense —
That it has no place where we are laughing
Which makes laughter a bright spot in darkness
So in all this mirth and light, what is there
But darkness and everywhere else, all around?
And who can fully laugh realizing this
Unless the laughing matter is so bright
It effectively does away with night?

Melangelical

It's all in a mixing bowl, as the years pass
They add to the mix, swirl in as bushes
Growing on the edge of the yard, burieds,
Berries I should say, popping everywhere
Like *confessurections.* I meant to say
Confections resurrected I confess
And don't entirely understand why this
Is happening though it's meaning seems clear.
They become *shrivelations* as I age
Revelations as I shrivel, I mean
More like last thoughts as I drift off to sleep
But carrying aromas of the stew
Somehow it's all *magnifideficient*
Sadly less than I wanted, wonderfully more

Old Man River

Along the river where my life took shape
Coming in chords that introduce my theme
I did some things that still will make me gape
The river took them like it was a dream
The past at times does seem to be unreal
And yet I know I stood there on the banks
The muddy waters hide all one can feel
Just forget it happened, and then give thanks
It's flowing and is not a dried-up creek
It would be hell to have one's life exposed
To dredge it all up now, how it would reek
A river's born of all that has been hosed
Mine's wide and long, and always near flood stage
On the bottom, spent remnants of my age

Sirens

I heard a voice as I rode the river
And engaged it in a laughing manner
Found much in common, more to deliver
Me to evil though, raising my banner
It was then that I heard another voice
In which they were excellencies of wit
I found I didn't need to make a choice
Either — I simply made both voices fit
Under one banner on my riverboat
It was then the third and fourth voices
Harmonized the river into a moat
I hit ground in a castle of choices
Beauty in every window calling me
Bones around me as far as I could see

Oil for the Core

All we have by the end is either numb
From the constant haranguing and friction
Or there's basic acceptance of the hum
Smoother to live by the interdiction.
Sure it's hard, but we also know it's right
Despite the shrill, threatening scream we hear,
The awful squeak that wails on day and night
As long as truth continues without fear.
The peace passing understanding, you reach
In long experience that turns to voice,
Giving good directions is how to teach,
One drives oneself after all, it's all choice
The body wears out, but the soul's designed
To see one's way through where others go blind.

It's not Abstract

It's not abstract when a variable
Proves to be a number that satisfies —
Unknown at first, then step by step until
Unmasked it's the answer no one denies
These are eureka moments in a proof
An algebraic function I can find
The right answer such that all doubt goes *poof*
And there's no doubt of truth in any mind
But outside math, all ideas are abstract
As clearly as one can prove anything
Someone will deny it outright as fact
Pluck it from flight and say it had no wing
Thinking well and clearly will make one free
But through the murk and muddle most can't see

Mirror Lake

Sometimes there's no wind, the lake's a mirror
It isn't like when the mind draws a blank
More like fulfillment, peace, without error
A sense of grace and knowing who to thank
You accept the process, the state of things,
The fact that you will die, the world in pain
Banal as it may sound, when a bird sings
It all makes sense. It only starts to wane
When you read the paper or watch the news
Insanity here, anger everywhere
While churches are struggling to fill their pews
You can't change a world where people don't care
But it can change you, if you see *the all*:
As calm understanding starts to snowball.

Blood Suckers

Someone has wheeled out the bloodsucking worms
On a cart next to me where now I wake
And see these leeches squirm on their own terms
No apologies for this nature — Take
Us as we are, they say and we'll suck
You dry without giving it a slight thought
As we don't think but live in bottom muck
Instinct being the only thing we've got —
I sit and look at them, wondering who
Would want to do such a thing to hurt me
Disgusting bands of muscle that just do
What they must to survive and cannot see —
Then a doctor comes, calls it a success —
I spewed them as I began to confess

Only the Truth

You are obsolete, the voice said to the truth
We do not need you anymore, that's true!
You're so far gone now like the word 'forsooth.'
We'll stick to facts now like the sky is blue.
Even though the blueness can be explained
Away, it's blue. We've better things to do
Like answer where's the snow and why it rained
And lay all the guilt on heads of a few
A whole new order's about to emerge
Only the truth is standing in the way
So this is why there needs to be a purge
Be careful how you think and what you say.
The voice went on and on, ranted and raved
But in the end, only the truth was saved.

Beyond the Fictions

Getting to the real truth, past saving face
Beyond the fictions where I'm not to blame,
I bow out, admit I couldn't keep pace
And take whatever comes including shame.
I sometimes project there is a state of mind
Clear of what inhibits, releasing me
To sheer peace of spirit, which is the kind
Of bliss where you accept all that you see —
I don't mean evil, because that's removed
The thing that breaks the heart it keeps in chains.
Free of that, though everywhere it be proved,
Good subtracts it and is all that remains.
Suddenly there's nothing that can't be done:
The mind I'd most want could I choose but one.

Landfill

Life's encapsulated in the ice pack,
Sound bites in lost files in a heap, each
A snowflake from snowfalls long ago, back
In core samples that can be used to teach
Here's a snippet caught on a microphone
And there's a photo in bitmap format
Very clear recording like a bleached bone
Though the picture's more an old *scrap dot dat*
Only the present resonates, not what
We collect. We have mountains of the past
But can't rebuild, like we're missing some nut
Or bolt. We dig things up that didn't last.
But now they inform us of what's to come
When our lives heaped become one huge cold crumb

The Bends

For beginners hearing their first deep poem,
I must consider those who have come along
Who sense the vastness from the ocean foam
And don't want me to simplify the song.
So into the deep end here from the shore
Wading the shallows down into the trench,
The crushing pressure's an image, no more.
But the siren singing's not just some wench;
Thank your mother, wrecked by an evil lord,
A Titan perhaps, yes, let's spice this verse,
Leave it half-baked but well done, since you're bored,
Explained in the end by some kind of curse.
That's it, come up for air, and rise too fast
So your blood will come to a boil at last.

Escaping the Honey Flower

I escaped the honey flower, its sweet
And sticky tendrils wouldn't let me go
I had to pull away, somehow defeat
The thing before it dissolved me. Slow
As it was, I felt it taking my soul
Little by little. I would wake from bed
Diminished by slight degrees, never whole
The flower bigger, waiting to be fed
I had to find a way to live, or die
The horrible death of fading away
So I made a pact with myself to try
To become poison to her, come what may
Which I did by just giving up my place
To one who likes getting spit in the face

Myth Maker

She walked out on him, though now they are friends
Though she never found out how he cheated,
never figured out all the lies he told
that had a way of keeping him at bay,
drove him from closeness in which they started,
filled him with worry and self-consciousness,
transmuted his heart into a facade
until she sensed the emptiness behind
and began by degrees to break away.
He could have stopped her if his heart were right.
She poured herself through the holes in the cup,
dripped away, dropped into a whole new life.
Now they talk, old friends who once shared a bond,
and he exudes the myth she let him down.

Where All Things Go

One day I fell out of the salt shaker
When it was shaken over mounds of meat
My crystal missed, thanks to the bad baker
Who didn't care to keep the kitchen neat
I sat there on the floor until one day
A wet mop put me in a dirty pail
Where I dispersed, having nothing to say
On the matter, but now I'll tell my tale
My life became ions, which has its plus
But its minus also — it was a wash
And as a chemical, I didn't fuss
I just reacted, no emotions — Gosh,
No — Actually, I went with the flow —
I'm in the ocean now, where all things go

Sunken in the Bay

We're in sunken ships deep in the bay
We're alive but no one can get to us
We tap on the hull with wrenches to say
Send help quickly, but no one makes a fuss
By the time they cut through, we'll be dead
So all just go about their work and lives
The sounds of tapping always in the head
Rescue abandoned after many dives
The harbor hums with noise of repair crews
But everyone hears our tap tap tapping
It goes on so constantly one could lose
One's mind — wrenches pinging, overlapping
Everyone calls for help, but there is none
And drop out to silence one by one

Don't Be Anything

Don't be anything, because some will try
To pull you from whatever you achieve
With whatever works, starting with a lie
Until you will voluntarily leave;
So don't even set out or make a move
In directions of trying to succeed,
You'll only find quicksand, which won't improve,
From which you won't be able to be freed.
Stay under the radar in all you do,
Don't try to shine or be more than you are;
Success is honey on the skin, where you
Will be tied down with an anthill not far.
Thus it is for serving truth anymore:
You come in peace; what greets you will be war.

Man on Earth

There's a man in the moon, we all knew that,
In harmonious open space, his clock
Runs perfectly, keeps tide on time, old hat
It's so well understood, there's just no talk
Of the universe having any flaw,
Only that it's running smooth as can be,
Obedient to all physical law
We can ascertain through all we can't see.
Against that backdrop, looking at ourselves,
It's clear by comparison there's a taint
In us, something dark; anyone who delves
Would say it makes the universe a saint.
So the man in the moon's good without doubt,
It's man on earth we should worry about.

Simple and Direct

Sometimes it comes to starting over what
Reached its pinnacle in another time
The words are there but the people are not
And our best substandard in their prime
So when all literature is compared
Later on by minds of highest learning
It may appear that this era was scared
To excel in art and lacked the yearning
But frankly that would be pearls before swine
As keepers of the flame light cigarettes
As all party and sleep past host and wine:
Ate and drank too much are the big regrets
Great art now is like talking to a child
Simple, direct is how it must be styled

Walking the Earth

In the ebb and flow of all I don't know
There comes from the waves something in a shell
It lands on a beach in sands white as snow
And I feel that it holds the fires of hell;
A portal to one who can't take the heat?
Who could it beckon when most run away?
Who is not repelled by evil so complete
One abandons hope to enter, as they
Say? I see on one side *terre* is engraved
And try to kick it back into the sea
It lodges between my toes and is saved
Could going barefoot mean the end for me?
Then I realize it's earth; around its shore,
Our hot heart, and the great unknown its core.
    4.21.17

Missing the Mark

For each degree I stray from what is real
I give up something of the truth to lies
It starts out innocuously in zeal
And ends up in distant fictions, the size
Of which astounds the mind, how fake things are.
We stand though with death staring down at us
To put the intolerable truth far
Away, to find comfort, what's the big fuss?
But there's fiction that's more evil than good
And virtual worlds that will take one's soul.
Step into darkness, but do as you should
Explore, test the spirits, but come back whole:
From light of truth to black evil's the range;
To see evil as benign is what's strange

Holy Relics

Imagine Michelangelo finding
The perfect marble slab for some great work
But saving it for years, never grinding
Or chiseling at all because a quirk
Makes him want to keep it always pristine
So it sits in his workshop, a wonder
In its own right, nothing like the Sistine
Chapel, but it's perfect with no blunder
Or blemish at all. It's like a notebook
Da Vinci never wrote or drew inside
Which had lovely white pages someone took
Time to hand make, a leather cover dyed
So well — both masters sensing perfection
That's akin to a kind of rejection

Glaring Simplicity

The right way to think things through, when it hits
Will fly through the population like fire
Leaving evil shattered in little bits
For gathering up, burning on a pyre
What will such thoughts look like? How will they come?
A boy called out the emperor's new clothes
A word is all it takes, the truth in sum
Added in the crucible to a rose
As dawn dispels darkness, so will this light
In glaring simplicity that we know
Is the truth on first hearing, that it's right
Then we're hostages freed from the sideshow
Why is what's obvious last to be said?
Count the lives saved but remember the dead

Light Fish

Light fish on trees keeping track of the times
Are invisible to most, but I see
One and gently detach it as it swims
Higher up to try to hide in the tree
These beings are objective and record
Events exactly as they now unfold.
It's all the living truth. We can't afford
To ignore witnesses like these who hold
The key to understanding our whole past.
Some are ancient; sadly some were destroyed
In our wars along the way, but at last
We know they're here. We should be overjoyed
But now, because I see them, I'm a threat —
I just release them, glad I'm in their debt.

39

In God's Diameter

I paint here from a glorious vision
Full of flashes of insight and wonder
Seeing it, what it lacks in precision
Is made up for in the peals of thunder
You can feel blasting out from overhead
You've been brought into this electric air
Like a charged particle back from the dead
Made newly alive as you are now aware
It is a seamless whole like one great thought
But now to question it, here come the fools
Looking for devices as they were taught
And to judge whether I've broken the rules —
A sonnet, iambic pentameter
Fourteen lines, rhymed, in God's diameter.

Stone Marker Garden

After all was said and done, we were sent
From the garden and made the least of it.
Compared to what it was, as it was meant
To be, fit for God, He wouldn't visit
Our poor excuse for a welcome mat.
Our disputes on how to improve our lot
Devolved to great wars that grew from a spat
To level and destroy what we had got.
Now I'm reading the myth of the wolf packs
Blowing down each kind of house built to stand,
Where friends die anyway; and soon life lacks
Love for the world's ways. To seek God's hand
In time we have left will clear weeds from the rock,
Create a garden the devil will stalk.

Wanderers

It shouldn't surprise me, since few read books
When I did, that there are so many lost
And living a life that no longer looks
For the real truth no matter what the cost
As time is running out. Well, so are they
Like the slime mold that never found the food
Aimlessly wandering the agar tray.
Those that do, explode in a whole new brood
Of veins like brain cells stretching in the dish.
Imagine a desert of longhorn skulls
And these are the living — each with a wish:
To not meet an end with vultures and gulls.
The free mind is the one that takes a leap
From the sand to the everlasting deep

Head of the Class

In our free class, who hates freedom can sit
And be disruptive, protest and complain
If they got their way, there would be a pit
To burn the books and all that they disdain
The first thing would be redesign the schools
Teach children the new ideas to believe
They must adhere to, not question these rules
Wear the uniform of the correct weave;
But in our free class, today there's a change
Those who love freedom, believers in God
Are asked not to speak, though that may seem strange.
But we want to hear from the meek and odd,
So if you've issues with that, drop the class:
You're already marked as one who won't pass

Light and Darkness

Imagine I see a light, and you don't
But you think you do, yet walk in the dark
No matter how I try to share, you won't
Be dissuaded and think you're on the mark.
Now continue to imagine you're wrong —
And continue to imagine I'm right —
The end is coming, and it won't be long
Before we find which one of us sees light
But it leaves no message for those behind
Except ones that are here to open eyes
And these are offset by another kind
That works to shut out light until one dies.
Not knowing what's beyond, it's hard to choose
The problem is if you choose wrong, you lose

Limiting the Unlimited

Let's post guards at the limits, at the wall
Of what we can know, and call it, *The End*,
Arrest anyone who mentions Saint Paul
Or sees through the wall darkly, to defend
The position that something lies beyond.
They *know* in part, but we know all in full
Though they have ability to bond
We'll just shout, *Religion's a lot of bull*
And at some point, we'll put them all in jail
But of course, we'll need to tie them to crimes
To question our truth is beyond the pale
We would crucify them in other times
What are we afraid of if nothing's there?
Why so worried if we haven't a prayer?

No Show

No music's accompanying the storm
We stand, watch it roll slowly from the west
Cellos and bass fiddles would be the norm
But silence, birds and sunbeams will do best
To accentuate by contrast the dark
Horizon now on us, ready to spill
And unleash what will more than leave a mark
Quiet moments, doldrums, dull, no drums, still
It feels like a huge buildup to a crash,
A boom that's not sounded, where is the thunder?
Expecting the winds to suddenly lash
And great forces to rend us asunder
But nothing comes. Just a few calm bird tweets
Playing songs that call us back to our seats

Overture

When it's all over, this is overture
From the beginning, it's been afterward
It's truth, not the words, that will long endure
My pen is mighty, but I have a sword
From our first steps, last rites are in the air
An ashen cross is marked on our forehead
Before we've begun to grow any hair
All of our lives, we think of ourselves as dead.
Life is the present moment of the past
Some give, while others take what they can't keep
The last will be first; the first will be last
The finish line is somewhere in the deep
We'll hit bottom, too late to hold our breath
And dream of shallows far away from death

Raised to Obey

When you look back at all the lies you bought
Like all the half truths science sold to you
All the supposed facts that you took as true
That you never once researched as you ought
You should wonder who you let form your mind
How did they rate to rise to such a height
To make you take what you didn't find
For yourself, not being sure it was right
Where are they more like spices in life's thick soup
Than main ingredients of meat from bone?
Did they seem so true that you were their dupe
Or maybe your friends said they liked their tone —
Strange: you thought through nothing yourself, a slave
To their creed, yet supposed you're free and brave

Heard on a Train

Sing the song the ocean is God, the salt
Water's His blood. It washes everything
Just smell that air! How could it be our fault
It's only natural to have a fling
We follow our hearts like the rivers flow
Sometimes we flood — one time we nearly drowned
But I prefer to think God didn't know
Even He answers to nature I found
You saw how I was laughed at by a priest
Who still tries to sell that Christ is God's son
He must not have seen a sunset out east...
...In Tampa anyway — that's a good one —
I have worshipped the sea since I found that shell
A conch that whistles proof there is no Hell.

The Man at the Fire

The man at the fire without hose or axe
Bucket or ladder, no training or truck
Said he was there just to write all the facts.
He watched as the whole thing burned to the ground
Then was a suspect for his lack of aid —
Blamed even, as investigators found
A pen in a socket, the sparks it made
Still there as charred marks, which they're calling luck
And with the pictures putting him at the scene
There's a good case for arson. Looks like proof.
A background check shows he was very keen
To cause evil. He only seemed aloof —
Now we hear fire shoots from his eyes and nose
And he says things only the devil knows

Relic Essence

The real disappears when the mind wanders
Like dry ice in hot air, soon it is gone
Regret will follow the one who squanders
His pocket of light, trades for night his dawn
And one day wakes to find himself alone.
One in hand is lost, two in bush now three
The life you knew in soft skin turns to stone
The lonely *I* returns, cut out from *We*.
It starts with boredom, apathy, and then
All we value gets put up on the block.
We fall asleep on our watch; then again
We choose to test old keys in a new lock
Except the new lock wasn't real, but took
All we had. I should say: all we forsook.

One Way

If I were a laser with even the most
Concentrated light, would I be as apt
To hit a dot miles away on a post
Without a steady hand that also mapped
The range to help me to not miss the point?
There aren't many ways to bring out the best
When every answer's looking to anoint
Itself the only way to pass the test
And eliminate the competition.
Sadly the truth is just hidden enough
To make every age a new rendition
Of not quite recognizing each new bluff.
Though we each have the same target in mind
We're gripped with true aim, or we're shooting blind.

Open Space

There's always an open space for a glint;
In the great distances, you'll see a flash
And know somehow you've been offered a hint.
From a slim angle, thin as an eyelash,
It's always there like a searingly bright
Small slit in fabric covering a star.
But the greater part still lies in the night,
Open spaces that abound near and far,
Empty of fiery posts that guide the soul,
Seemingly bereft of all that reflects,
Where beings have eyeless slits as a mole
Tunneling blind to light and its effects.
The open space within is all that counts
As darkness spreads from which no light will bounce.

Core Puzzles of the Deity

The core puzzles of the deity, true
Blood that carries us all: Those who sense
Perfect full spectrum's reach in partial hue
Blessed with peace beyond words in the immense
Ultimacy that applies to each soul;
Those who doubt, who still have time to believe
In life's long process of becoming whole
Though losses mount from which there's no reprieve;
And those in complete denial, at a wall
that an unseen hand could be on the move,
Hard against faith in any form, who all
Live a form of faith for what they can't prove.
Truth loves investigation, so look deep:
You might just join the faithful who've made the leap.

Einstein on a Swing

Einstein's on a swing, rotating. His toes
touch the ground as a guide. He's lost in thought.
His motions appear to have a rhythm,
a shape suggestive of an equation
that would explain them. But one cannot tell
whatever it is that is on his mind,
however he might see or sense the grout
in the seams of the seemingly seamless
in a form only he can formulate.
He just seems lost in swinging on the swing,
the capillaries in his closed eyelids
invisible to us in blinding light.
He knows the sky just seems blue, and art's truth
dangles brilliance and mystery in one

47

At Hart Crane's Grave

The thunderous undulating waves roar
Along the coast, but out there, it's all still
The crypt, three fourths the planet, has no door
So it's an open casket, waked at will
In burials at sea, there are words said
Here, over his own grave, perhaps he spoke
Before jumping in and joining the dead
More likely, to speak would feel like a joke
But no last words from a man or hermit
No poem to express all the reasons why
Into love's hands and without a permit
Is a sadness, a kind of Quaker sigh
No marker, no buoy, except it's well marked
I lived, I died, and earth is where I've parked.

Following Locals

I saw a lizard on a desert beach
And followed as it scampered to a cave
Somewhere within, it turned into a leech
As the tide filled the chamber with a wave
Gasping for breath in air pockets above
I could feel the leech lock onto my heel
As my blood drained, oddly, I could feel love
Love for everything though I was the meal
Whatever would eat me, I was its friend
And right then the leech had grown long and fat
It finally let go, my blood at an end
I sunk to the bottom, empty and flat
I get this lots when I travel abroad
When I follow locals looking for God

Goat's Clothing

I'm serving good, he stated, horns on head
Don't mind my goat body and cloven toe
Just follow me, and you'll be fine, he said
The world will be yours, the star of the show
And all you ever dreamed of will be yours
Then you'll mix with other stars of the age
Our enemies will be ignored, just bores
Who none pay to see, who can't find the stage
You'll be in the center of the mainstream
And I have the power to keep you there
You'll get used to it, it won't be a dream
You'll have the world by both the tail and hair
Just sell me your soul, I'll send you the bill
Otherwise life is work and all uphill

The Question

I want to put a question in your brain
Is it allowed? If not, who says I can't?
Do you say no, or does your government?
To both I'd ask, what damage could it do?
Can minds in the shape of question marks,
Always probing, wanting to find the truth,
Really pose a danger, threat to the world,
Or is it more about what they might find?
And what could that be that cuts questions off?
What could one possibly find that's so bad?
Or might it be good like food for the soul
Establish one higher than bonds can hold?
In any case, I don't want trouble
So I won't ask the question after all.

Free Through it All

In school, they showed us histories of war,
And part of the assignment was to see
That this repeats itself, for to the core
We're born to trouble, that's how it will be.
But at the same time, we were tasked with this:
That of keeping ourselves free through it all.
If enough will sustain it, it can't miss
And our birthrights and our freedoms won't fall.
But swirling within like a poison pill
There's a sense that the broth has turned bitter;
One taste is enough, and here comes the bill...
Tear it up, and it just becomes litter.
They want to kill us but get us to pay,
Make everything free, take freedoms away.

The Archivist

The archivist in the old dusty room,
With dim light and a basement's musty smell,
Is advanced in years and can feel his doom
Approaching, and he has so much to tell.
He knows where everything is, why it's there
In ways that none could learn to take his place.
The knowledge to be lost hangs in the air,
The archives themselves come in second place.
But important as he is, what he knows
Is not sought out, he sits there all alone.
Seeing one stack to the next, it all flows
In his mind like a kind of great unknown.
I notice as I walk around the aisles
A most amazing thing: he often smiles.

Photo Finish

From the second they lay you in the pan
It's about developing, coming clear,
Will you get the picture, become a man,
Or will the full exposure be unclear?
It's a chemical concoction and light
With positives and negatives to crop.
There's enlargement and focus, and the right
Time to shed light, let it resolve and stop.
Then it bathes in fixer, then hangs and dries...
From metaphor to time in the darkroom,
This is parallel, one captures, one dies:
Frame, hang one up; the other gets its tomb.
Welcome to life, to your photo finish
Time gets you, but this will not diminish.

Road Rage

A rainbow of all inclusiveness hung
Over the road. As we all stopped our cars
To look, we felt lucky to be among
Those who saw white light divided. The scars
Smoothed over in the conceptual light;
We felt certain this was the means to heal
The world. Now we had it to make things right.
So we resumed driving, thinking it real;
Then racing, honking, cutting off began,
Which refracted color stripes out of black,
Described as natural instincts of man.
Some saw then this rainbow had its drawback:
It appeals to the mind but lacks in law,
Seems an answer first, then shows its deep flaw

A *Flashing Brilliance*

From behind in the nursing home, his head
Seemed so white and flat, almost like a screen
To watch his show before heading to bed;
What he saw were things you've never seen
He had lightning, a great power of mind
But looking at his skull, you wouldn't know
Where it could have come from, like did he find
An inspiration and make the force grow?
But whatever it was has left him now
He's not the man he was by any means
He left his power in words, took no bow
But settled in to getting served his greens
Now quietly gathered around his grave
Distant thunder reminds us what he gave

Bouncing off the Wall

We just throw balls on this side of the wall
They obey all laws of physics all day;
Calculate gravity, the rate they fall:
Force converts to distance on the fairway.
But still I know there's more going on here
Than can be scientifically explained:
How high my spirit soars when she is near;
How deep it hurts to learn that love was feigned.
But the measurements of things in action
Is impressive; man should be very proud
He can take whole things and make a fraction;
Put both fire and ice in a mushroom cloud.
But all he knows, he doesn't know it all
Only how things bounce this side of the wall

Starting to Turn

I sit here feeling like a wheel of cheese
Aging too far to be considered peak
Not quite overripe to cause a disease
But perhaps only for those who might seek
A taste that is strange, a special palate
A willingness to get out and explore
Take the horse but leave the polo mallet
This is not a game where you can keep score
And when you ride from town to town, you find
Local distinctions, perhaps some fine wine
Tie the horse and get away from the grind
It's an out-of-the-way place without a line
Where you find that cheese just starting to turn
Excellence at this level's hard to learn

Transcendent Orienteering

Poetry is a cure of the mind.
   ~ Wallace Stevens

Transcendent orienteering, you start
After arrival after many years
Through careful study of matters of heart
Including gray areas and your fears
Imagine you've grown wise and now the whole
World surrounds you in madness. This is where
You begin mapping a path for the soul
Your success will breed more, however rare
This is not about which books you have read:
One's life itself means more to make the choice
To find a way to get beyond the head
And not just make a noise but have a voice.
Where there's cogent integrity you'll find
A transcendence where madness can unwind

Wanting to Love

This wanting to love is a cry for peace,
To touch you, take away my fear of death,
That all the madness in the world will cease,
And I'll be in your arms feeling your breath.
To have your heartbeat, not the sounds of trains;
To have time, the whole day to lie in bed,
Would energize my spirit the world drains
To wordlessly feel what you haven't said...
I know nothing can be changed overnight,
I stand in constant onslaught of the rain,
But the clouds dissipate when you're in sight
Like an old love song with a sweet refrain.
Against a backdrop of war and despair
I want to run my fingers through your hair.

The Kite

Imagine you are summed up in a flash
A moment captures and defines your soul
In a metaphor. Say one day you crash
Your car, not your fault, there was a big hole
In the street, but the snapshot as you walked
From the scene, arms spread, shirt out like a kite
Portrays you in new light, you never talked
Of it then, but later recalled a flight
Where you saw the accident far below,
So you became a kite for a short while
And that's what you'll always be, even though
It paints you in dim light being senile
But who can see you any other way?
You're now the kite no matter what you say

A Joyful Sound

I made a glad sound, and someone said stop
So I wrote the conflict down in a verse
And published it. In a few days, a cop
Appeared and said I had made matters worse
I was taken but couldn't plead my case;
Became a prisoner. A dirty cell
Was my home for months. I lost weight. My face
Looked older; my health soon went to hell
The only sounds I made were in great pain;
But they did nothing. They hoped I would die
Or at the very least would go insane
Which would go a long way to explain why
I'd reacted the way I had that day...
You make a joyful sound, you're going to pay.

More Than Stars Can Explain

A series of accidents centers me
To spend my whole life in an inner world
Panning for truth, improving by degree,
Coming to shine the way oysters are pearled.
This is not some cheap glaze bought at the store
Swabbed on to cover, to smooth over fault;
It's a natural process, and there's more:
Oceans with the same percent of salt
As one finds in us, as if it's our home,
Or was in some beginning in a shell,
Unless we're the template for salt in foam,
You can't tell much, only there's more to tell.
The mind's much more than the parts of the brain,
The cosmos is more than stars can explain.

Oceans of Spirit

Hard to think but in oceans of spirit,
with great skies above the waves and even
higher endless space leading up to God,
we are the bottom feeders, things that crawl
at the lowest point on the spirit scale,
which, as we see it, is the great center,
like the solar system: we are the sun,
and all things tend around us, even God.
We're told that it's the other way around
but somehow can't collectively abide
to soar, circle and serve a greater Lord.
Dumb fish fill the oceans, dull birds the skies;
beyond that, there's star-studded emptiness.
It's all so clear to see behind closed eyes.

Original Sin

Sin is not original; it's not new
It started when the whole world first began
Some say there's no such thing, depending who
You talk to, but it's in the heart of man,
And it has been always been there since the first
Which is why it's called original, and
Whether mankind seems good or at its worst
Sin's always in play, is dealt in your hand
But it comes down to you to make a choice,
To follow good or evil, God or man;
To leave God out, without His word and voice,
Only man's way is left, since time began;
Hopeless without truth, the world creates its own,
And ignores the tablets written in stone.

Phoenix Rising

The imagined one who changed the nation
Built by progressives as a poster child
Starting point for total saturation
Is no more a danger, but kind and mild
And now with a toehold, it wants in schools
Remove the values of two thousand years
To redo education to new rules
Let anything go with what each sees and hears;
So for imagined wrongs on very few
Though yes there have been incidents far flung
A whole generation gets a redo
And who speaks against it loses their tongue
The truth's at stake, and ready to be burned
The Phoenix rises from a death that's earned.

Pit Driven

I feel like I can help, then like I can't
And imagine the world evolving to
A new age of clear thought, no one to rant
Ridiculous ideas and be one who
Is followed, least not by half of the world;
Civil war of left and right at an end,
Justice and truth again flying unfurled
In a flag all are ready to defend
But the question is, where did it go wrong?
How did they think such bad ideas were true?
Like going by foggy lyrics of a song
And turning God's green earth into a zoo
The human mind's an engine; fueled by sin,
We drive ourselves into the pit we're in

Spinning Down

The winds we whip up in life stir the mind
Make waves we ride until we gain sea legs
Over many years we begin to find
Ourselves encrusted but walking on eggs
Vessels most likely to burst are not boats
We reach old age still spinning from the ride
Remembering how we sowed all our oats
We dream to go out again on the tide
But tides have turned, and it's time to turn in
We try and retry, then tire and retire
We come to an end near where we begin
Watching embers like years spark from the fire
We can't get too excited, that is past,
And spin down slowly to a point that's vast

For a Pittance

One day you're in charge, the next being shot
From trusted ally to traitor of state
Where a joke of a trial proves you were bought
Cuffed, shamed and silenced, you're led to your fate
When this kind of system's beaten, some root
Somehow survives since it's deep in the heart
War may get the neck from under the boot
But the next generation takes the start
Of the growth of the insidious vine
As something in need of personal touch
The young don't remember, and see a sign
In flawed ideals and fight for them as such
The heart of man is a bottomless hole
And for a pittance gladly sells his soul

The Inglorious That Was

My friends, it's man who's digging his own grave
all the time; man who forgets what he's done;
Man who repeats his mistakes, who can't save
Himself, yet overlooks God's only son
Back and forth in our hearts, we come to terms
With truth only by centering the mind
It isn't long before we face the worms
And face the final truth to which we're blind
This does not mean we've no time left to live;
Only that we live in a different way;
It's not what we receive but what we give
Where's freedom's measured in how we obey.
The sermon ended, and we all went home,
Surrounded by a world becoming Rome

Presumptions

We didn't come here knowing how we're here,
And yet we're so quick to believe we do
With faith we say there's no faith, think we're clear
Presume, without knowing, we came from goo:
Primordial slime, a mixture no lab
Can make, but they call it the building blocks
Of life, point to space and begin to blab
Of life everywhere on all those dead rocks
This is not science, I mean, where's the proof?
They say there's no God, but have faith in this?
If you don't subscribe, they go through the roof
Betray, crucify you, after a kiss.
Some things aren't known, so why should I agree
To stop seeking truth based on some decree?

The Raving

So I ponder weak and weary, so what?
Who cares of forgotten lore, answers there
Would be surpassed by now. By what my gut
Tells me, a raven isn't everywhere
Reminding me of doors closed in the past.
I understand that life itself must end
And continues, though my own will not last
Nor is it something I would seek to bend
Nevermore from beak or mouth, it's the same
Every second is the last of its kind
You aren't eternal just by having fame
The search should really be for peace of mind
And when past losses stack to pull you down
Recall the three crosses outside of town

Starting with Nothing

From details left out of God's grand design
We have no answer except to believe —
Faith in such a way to not need a sign,
Not indulge the scientific pet peeve
Creation has no proof; build life from zilch,
Declare life when the *ingredients* are found?
Where's mystic mystery when you can filch
It away in theories with little ground?
The picture's really not so incomplete
That we need big bangs. It doesn't explain
How things appeared before all that great heat
That blew, scattered galaxies and brought rain
Absolute nothing's the real mystery
Start there, then explain any history.

Siren Song

The sultry voice with accents from the shore
Calls to me though I'm lashed hard to the mast
A lovely timbre that cuts to my core
I've flashed over from wanting to get past
In new blood and spirit, my aim's to stay
To break what binds me and bond with her there:
Somewhere, just follow her whispers. The bay
Is deep, my anchor chain's made from her hair
I don't know why, but the more I close my eyes,
The fewer tears: suffering disappears;
I'm in another world and hear no cries
And though bones are piled high, I have no fears.
Then her singing fades; I'm not on her beach
As senses return when she's out of reach

Cracking the Code

Turn around, I said to men in battle
But they kept on fighting for the great cause
It didn't matter they died like cattle
Slaughtered in suspension of higher laws
Now causes are forgotten, laws in place
But there is talk; they're restless in the ranks
They have it wrong in things like hate and race
And don't believe in anything like tanks
But tanks will roar on hills when war will come
The men will train to fight and learn to die
The numbers of the dead will make one numb
And each side thinks it guards truth but will lie
This sign will stand there, posted on the road
Turn back, it says, if you can crack the code.

Holey Tree

Over the hill across the water, God
Is talking to one chosen to receive
What He has deemed worthy in good time. Odd
That He didn't pick me, for by His leave,
Knee bent and scarcely looking in His eye
He could change me further, heal me to hear
His commands, give me great strength from on high
Even to make me forget what I hold dear
But someone else has had his name chosen
Makes me wonder if I've ignored His call
There have been a few times I felt frozen
To make a move myself for fear I'd fall
Now I'm riddled with life's bugs, an old tree
Whose shade's no good should prophets come near me.

Phases of Man

I ran so fast, my current touched the moon
The boost spun it, the far side came to view
Full but odd to see even at high noon
No one understood or knew what to do
The ocean tides behaved the same, no change
Except we were seeing the other face
Still, there were objections in a wide range
Some wanted it back but couldn't embrace
A plan, except perhaps to use the bomb:
Having seen movies where an asteroid
Was blown off course so life again grew calm.
But this was no collision in the void
So I ran again, fixed it in one stride
And damn if most didn't want the dark side.

Orpheus

The harp: limited sonic inclusion
In the full repertoire, still has its place
In myth, Orpheus and his delusion,
Came close as one could come in his case
To giving gods reason to suspend rules
Winning a chance that preys on human flaw
Like getting flayed by Apollo: who duels
Loses, but the attempt reveals the law,
And the spirit that holds itself higher
And is; transcends even in God's own eyes
Yet one still has to submit to the fire
And big as the soul is, come down to size
With song so rare that Gods are moved to tears
Looking back on beauty's the least of fears

Tyranny of Submission

Why would anyone want good things hidden
Act like they never existed at all
Cast them aside and make them forbidden?
Line up their defenders against the wall?
This is like telling trees not to bear fruit
Or they will be uprooted and then burned
When tyranny prospers, the truth is moot
To hell with all where honor is concerned
So for a time good things are cast aside
They rise up high who toe the narrow line
The fat king says he's better, so abide
And ride out the days, and you'll be fine
Then his son takes over, and it gets worse
Your submission wastes the land like a curse

The Black Slime

Another day escaping the black slime
That creeps along and gets in all our hair
Once it gets you, it's a matter of time
It takes you or it doesn't; nothing's fair
I've had brushes with it, watched it take friends
And family away from me. In war
It covers whole battlefields as it wends
Its way as if dancing as cannons roar
But all that mud's just blown up bits of men
And all their blood drains into No Man's Land
Soon green carpets of grass appear again
The slime retreats but maintains its command
The farms grow lovely with the trenches gone
Gardens transfused with underlying spawn

Grandfathered

I know the way, said the stump. It was true;
Once a tree for more than a thousand years
The stump did know the way but couldn't do
Squat as all the people listened to seers
Who garbled speech to code, for being stumped
Though they sounded quite profound, they were lost
And neither led nor followed, merely lumped
Their forecasts in a book sold at high cost.
Then one day a man sat on the old stump
And sensed what the stump was trying to say
Felt ancient wisdom in the sawed-off bump
Yet the man was not looking for the way
His job was to kill whatever might know
But since the tree had died, he let it go

Reanimagined

Can you take this skeleton, these bones please,
And fill it with some new organs right here?
We carved away all the live flesh with ease,
It took two hundred years, but always felt near,
Finally we have the perfect set of bones.
There's no proof though these organs will survive,
Other attempts failed, we still hear the moans.
The being of the bones was happy alive,
But we kept at it, slowly pecked away
And bit by bit removed its very core.
Now what it will replace becomes cliché,
Obsoleted like some forgotten lore.
Give it new morals with your magic wand
Tied down to here, severed from the beyond.

Protocols

The protocols are here to stay in force
Not that there will be no issues, but when
There are, you'll have followed the rules, of course
Helmets won't prevent breaking legs, but then
Without the headgear, it might have been much worse
And protocols are there for good reason
Long ago, kids bumped heads and cried, no nurse
Was present; now they're signed for the season
And enforce the bylaws to the letter
Parents get the handbook and have to sign;
We don't keep score either, which is better;
Losing can't exist in our grand design
Our great hope's that war can be a safe space
Amazing we say it with a straight face

In the Brook

All sorts of stray thoughts, a long school of fish
Passes along, and one gets on my hook
At first it feels like I've gotten my wish
But the next thing you know, I'm in the brook
I'm one with my thoughts as always, and yet
As I'm swarmed and nipped at in the deep bay
I feel I'm drowning for one I can't get
And haul myself out to call it a day
But then I see the pond rings where I swam
And something familiar beneath the glass
Connected again, it's as much *I am*
As separate, like twin photons without mass
In two places at once. *Nothing at all*
Seems distant, impossible to recall.

Where is There Nothing?

Where is there nothing? Please show me the place
Is there nothing after I move a chair?
Even in the vacuum of open space
There's width and breadth, and here on earth there's air
So where's nothing? Is it where the soul goes
Because after a body dies, we hold
It in memory while we can, which shows
Something's in us, but soon we too are cold
But that's not nothing; it's not made of thoughts
Billions of us together, all minds combined
Create a picture out of tiny dots
And call it nothing. Hell, it's even signed.
So where is nothing? Not sure if you care
But I went where it was, and it wasn't there.

Destination Not Oblivion

I guess I'm going somewhere pretty soon
I'm ruling out oblivion. I know
That *nothing's* not an option, like the moon:
A dark side lunar afterlife? Hey, let's go!
What happens, some half-witted guy declares
There's nothing, and it infects the next mind?
Forget great theologians. Who cares
To follow lines of thought, see what you find;
Perhaps you might read a book, take a class,
Rather than simply parrot what you hear
If it's not true, then you should take a pass
But if it is, isn't there more to fear
From thinking wrong what should be thought out well?
Not finding the real truth; that should be hell

Crane in the Wake

Hart Crane jumped ship after serving green fruit
Launched into the strait like unfinished lunch
Permitted himself voyage, got the boot
And left what looms in his words as a hunch
There's a city, transcendent in the sky
Some poets pulse their pizzicato there
Alluring, cogent strains, not asking why
But answering as waves, wind in one's hair
Crane stood on what he rendered, full of holes,
Tendered resignation, one final leap
Off signs of symmetry, inklings of goals
Not reached, but he came close and touched the deep
From where we prize even the shards of shells
And what cleanses all of personal hells

Cellular

We're each a connection to a network
Limited by the allotment of light
Doomed to blow out at the tiniest quirk
We're glowing wisps in vacuums in the night
Taking all in at once, we've a dull sense
That arrogantly we come to think is clear
Then snake our own ways through life like remnants
Of telegraph wires out in the frontier
The network meanwhile pours out from its leaks
Of billions disconnected: conscious specks
In fiber optic valleys at their peaks
Noose of our own lightning around our necks
We're open hydrants gushing in unknowns
On hold, talking to ourselves on our phones

Fearing What's Real

Those things our instruments cannot detect
Must not exist, we don't know where to look
For fantasy, which would be our defect
To think it's real because it's in a book.
But some matters go deeper to the heart,
And isn't just inside the breast of man
But guided in truth sensed not to be art
Rooted in good but somehow gets a ban.
But we cannot discern them in this scope.
What spectrum can elude our radar now?
Why must politics try to erase hope,
Control man's heart and soul no matter how?
Because they fear what's real but can't be seen,
Obscenely adverse to what is just serene

Nothing and Knowledge

I can't accept or convey emptiness:
If there's nothing, there is nothing to say.
The world's experiencing its umpteenth mess
Over whether there's more than just one way.
Hard factual data takes one so far,
Which leads to a dead end in this regard;
Removing all doubt just creates a scar.
You see it in false scientists turned hard
Against honest methods that left the door
Open for questions that swirl out of range
Believing without proof is at the core
Of religion: (faith without facts. How strange!)
Is it not all one giant miracle?
If nothing else, that seems empirical.

Illusion Battle

A chip off the old hologram is whole
If you peer into it: the rest is there
Just as the one action reveals the soul
It's one turn just as one's whole life is where
Some come to see it as a spinning top
In slower motion of the day by day
Or better, a gyroscope that won't stop
As long as guidance systems show the way
But rip that from a rocket, and it goes
Off course, spins totally out of control.
The same for us: an entelechy knows
The way and operates within as soul
But without truth, it's broken from the start
It looks whole but conceals pieces of heart

Fiber Optic Obit

By having a smart phone and following
The impetus of mind to switching apps
At every thought, that phone is swallowing
Us while right there we're sucking on its paps
It grows from play to a full-time routine
From mindless task to game, always engaged
Phone always in hand, looking at a screen
The mind no longer free to think but caged
Check weather, mail, traffic, then make a call
Make a note, get a message and reply
Like a leaf that can't reach ground in its fall:
Click the video link to watch it fly.
Remember when the mind alone was joy?
Now that's all being sucked out by a toy

Brave Articulation

Perhaps the hand sprayed over in the cave
Interpreted as saying, *I was here*
Is not any signature but a brave
Articulation of something held dear
That if brought to light would lead to one's death
Cave becoming last refuge in the land
To create this art and safely draw breath...
Rebellion is the image of the hand
For it's easy to find who it fits
So this gesture's in fact the tour de force,
When discovered, tests authority wits:
There is no matching hand to name the source
It could be anyone, but no one's named
As art gives all a hand to stay unblamed

Repeating Realities

Fractals never end as they're magnified
The same as atoms become galaxies
It's always true as we look far and wide
We see the repeating realities
Where anything becomes a metaphor
For something else in the grand scheme of things.
The veins of leaves are rivulets that pour
Through landscapes seen from space, the same as springs
To mind when lightning flashes run their course:
All things flowing jagged, natural, complete;
Whether at light speed, or much slower force,
Instants to eons, the patterns repeat
Veins in bodies fan out the same within
Oceans from high altitude look like skin

Let Them Have the World

Let them have the world. Who'd recommend that
if they didn't already own the place?
Fact is, the planet has never been ours
but is always in the control of the mad,
the angry, the greedy and power crazed
who keep us in a bottle without holes,
taxing us for stale air that is on loan.
But letting them have it doesn't matter
and nothing's ever changed, so why bother?
Just remember this: they can never have
the one thing that matters: they have the world,
but we have the truth they can't take away,
Which has them just where God wants them to be:
In a pig's mouth the apple of His eye!

In Different Handwriting

I go to sleep in different handwriting
The style of an embedded mind inside
Released to take the pen without fighting
I give it up, get taken for a ride
Sliding into completely letting go
The cogencies more lucid than awake
Make some new kind of distant sense you know
A kind of hidden spirit one can't fake
Its world is brighter but more vaguely stirred
With sharp edges that don't cut but direct
Point with a strange song like a kind of bird
That appeals to soul, not the intellect
Hieroglyphics without Rosetta Stone
Mystery that's compelling to the bone

Peripheral Extinction

By the time I'd risen high in the ranks
And met all the big names in Hollywood
I'd long since lost clear and honest grasp, thanks
To a swelled head that brought about no good.
I was one of those who lost all of me;
My soul was replaced by what's called winnings
That ate me up; I was no longer free,
Proving dead ends aren't all new beginnings.
I found myself at wit's end of my rope;
Hands too full to pull free from the treat jar,
I fizzled out in last glimmers of hope
And found good reasons to live in my car
Time is so short, so I'm saying so long
Dim lights drizzle to black, end my swan song

The Coward

Grown brave enough to say the stupid things
That none would ever stand for years before
Grown brave by numbers as a chorus sings
So out of tune though, it's hard to ignore
Grown brave by poor understanding to say
What cannot fly with the most basic test
Condemn the past because it's yesterday
And stand there looking as dumb as the rest
Grown brave to brush all common sense aside
Declare what makes no sense to get a rise
Lie when questioned, it may not fly, but glide
It will and grow to twenty times its size
Do what's not taught to little girl or boy
Grow brave enough not to build but destroy

New Eden

My name is Adam, and I have a plan
To match and go beyond the New Green Deal
Make a perfect world, a garden for man,
You'll see it has universal appeal.
The first thing is we'll build a giant dome
Over the whole nation, from coast to coast
We'll control the weather in our new home.
But here's what you'll love about it the most:
There won't be need for clothes of any kind.
We'll all be as we were before first sin
With no shoes, hats, cars, phones or planes, we'll find
Life much simpler. Pass the bill to begin;
Throw that socialist New Green Deal away,
Let's sit and eat forbidden fruit all day.

Hammerhead

My hammerhead alter ego drops its guard
The world of the deep moves in for the kill
I catch on pretty quick, which isn't hard
As I re-emerge with instinctive will
To start hammering again with my mind
Driving back a sea of remorseless things
They're furtive and sly, as one hides behind
A harmless boulder, then suddenly springs
But is sprung upon itself and devoured.
Master of imaginary domains
It's said in the real world I'm a coward
But I survive my own fears, which takes brains
I watch the endless dance leave me alone
And everything gets eaten to the bone

Noontide

I will take you as far as fourteen lines
Can go, and do as much as words can do
In that short span of wide open confines
That can be more a jungle than a zoo
A small space can be wild; the water hole
Draws all species as they all need to drink
Stand back and see the pixels of your soul
The central force that describes how you think
Like Nietzsche's Higher Man calls from a cave
A beggar, magician and shadow wait
Many voices to one; close up they rave
But step back, hear the outline of your fate
The water's drying up, and it's your turn
Your enemies wait in the high sun's burn

Same Old Song

She had a sublime voice until the song
Ended, and in the silence of the air
Voiced her opinion, not knowing how wrong
She was, how strident, biased and unfair.
He was so handsome with teeth white and straight
Said his lines to make one cry, but off set
He ground his axe and was strung out on hate
Like some political marionette.
She had her chorus with one chalk-scratch voice;
He had his army of puppets in tow
They told the same tale like there was one choice
Revealing how much they all didn't know:
Whatever you do well, just do the thing
Like shut up and act, or shut up and sing.

Call the Mighty Forward

Call the mighty forward, let's count the days
They each have left before they hit the grave
A few surprises here. Everyone pays,
And in last seconds, some pray for a save
But it's all adding up to the same thing,
That even the mighty in their full shine
Glowing in the news, filling minds, all sing
The same tune before the truly divine
And it's woefully off key to be sure
By every measure, these are all sold souls
But fine print promised them they would endure
And would get them all when they'd reached their goals
Then in hindsight, look to their mighty past
From bonfire to dust storm, a desert vast

Playing My Horn

Again I'm asked to come and play my horn
Which is a herald, the news on the street
I keep ringing my bell, and you are born
The town crier until you take your seat
Now in the assembly, the vote has come
You're all grown up and asked to make a choice
Your party looks at you, your conscience numb
You filibuster, no one hears your voice
Now I put both my horn down and my bell
Throw my hands up in the air and declare
Quite simply, quite loud, that all is not well
Now you are old, and you think it's not fair
You survey your past, far too late to change
You listen to me like I'm out of range

Slow Funeral Pyre

We're waiting for our number to be called
There comes a point we know it's coming soon
It may be that we're starting to grow bald
Those in front of us falling in a swoon
They're put at a table, the final stage
We weave baskets, nurses talk down to us
Like we're children, never a sign of rage
At the table, it looks like a stalled bus,
The passengers frozen, nothing to say
Looking through each other, not in the eyes
At their destination, the same each day
For my basket, I've chosen a large size
I'm hoping it will take me years to make
Then set me afire in it on some lake

Utopian Rude Awakening

We took a vote that everything be free
No surprise it passed, it sounded so good
They made us all think, *What's in it for me?*
But it knocked down institutions that stood
For hundreds of years, made solid by those
Who worked hard, believed in honest earning
And in God from whom every blessing flows;
But He didn't exist, we were learning,
So if we gave the state complete control
In turn it would take care of all our needs
We came to find too late we sold our soul
On every back a parasite now feeds
Now there's less, more costly and badly made:
We lost everything in a *free* upgrade.

The Best Arrangement

The premise here's not to say there's a God
But to ask who are you to say there's not?
As just a belief you state, it's odd
It's pressed as fact to suppress any thought
That contradicts it when there's room to doubt.
We all stand on what we know to be true
But what's right should also not be left out
Like leaving some things for the heart to do
The best arrangement is let us be free
To ask questions and find truth for ourselves
Not easy if we're just allowed to see
What a government permits on the shelves.
When ideas aren't just denied but are blocked
Look how life flourishes when it's unlocked

Holy Roller

I'm deciding whether heaven exists
It's up to me and whether I believe
I get to choose its attributes from lists
And say who will stay and who gets the heave;
As it is, I've almost made up my mind,
If there's a God, dividing what He does
From what He doesn't, is He mean or kind
And is He the same as He always was
Is the main straw we have for the scarecrow
How I fill it makes a limber or stiff
Spirit, caring or too aloof to know
But whether He exists is the big *If*
If I say He doesn't, there goes heaven!
I'm rolling for it now! Come on Seven!

Puppets in the Dark

The comfort in numbers, those who agree,
With whom you subscribe as a magazine
Creates a sense you must be right. You see
As someone else does who thinks he has seen
So now take a look at reality
And ask yourself how much it might be skewed
If absolutes are not your cup of tea
And just the cause matters, maybe you're screwed,
Misled as far as what eternity means,
But again, you live their values and stand
For what they do, everyone like machines
Owned and operated by the Black Hand
Perhaps you don't believe in that extreme
Your strings go into the fog, it would seem

Spent on Charon

Like an obol in grease where a finger
Guides me as Eurydice through a haze
I don't so much follow as much as linger
As if tailgate slipstreaming through the maze
Floating like an oven aroma lifts
Where I don't even need to use my eyes
Carried out of hell by one of the gifts
Of love in how its music never dies
Already dead I look back as I will
Trusting what's in front to keep me on track,
Having come so far for me, way downhill
Now the way's up where there's no looking back
A curse that self-fulfills back to such worth
Love's still the one chance to reach second birth

True Seers

What prophets raised delivered three wise kings
Which suggests it was wisdom lost on most;
Such truth is like Braille for the blind, and things
The bumps reveal lead to signs on a post
Though most choose not to learn to see and hear
Ignoring predictions for the long haul.
It still stays true through centuries, what's clear
Through scripture, but most won't see it at all;
Yet there's no fear the message will be lost,
And though most miss it, the true light still shines.
Though ignorance is astounding, the cost
Huge, and the blind world ignores the signs,
God pours full strength what we dilute to gist...
And I'm worrying my point will be missed.

Nowhere to Hide

Truth there's no bending the world tries to twist
Kill and bury what only grows back strong
Deny, defy with nostrils smoking mist
A tantrum, yes, with an army and song
A kind of control that's out of control
Which has no need of getting the facts straight
It just takes a crowd, and you're on a roll
Whip them up with lies, and promise them bait
A feeding frenzy on blood of the rich
You can't succeed, so you should get stuff free
Then force the religious to dig a ditch
To be their grave because they won't agree
Such paradise needs prisons alongside
It gets so perfect there's nowhere to hide

Feeding the Multitudes

I dreamed my life's work all fit in one book;
At the presentation point before God,
It fell from my hand into a small brook
Where a fish brought it back, which I found odd
I thought it might survive the fire if wet
So I didn't shake it or wipe it dry
I hadn't gotten to the Lord quite yet
So I flipped through my book and heaved a sigh
The pages were all clean, completely blank
The brook dipping washed away my life's work
I approached with nothing, and my heart sank
Next I observed the fish suddenly perk,
Surface, recite all my work to the Lord,
Then get thrown in fire as hungry crowds roared

Taps

Scanning my spigots to see what I've tapped
You'll find them, still dripping, on many things
But the one that's stuck in me has me sapped
I'm beginning to lose count of my rings
My books were all tapped and fairly well drained
Years ago. The taps are dry on the vine
The withered look of the shelves is not feigned
The vampire spigots sucked every last line
Gathering strength from the blood of these books
I began to tap people and places
Nothing would stop me as I got my hooks
Into it all, touching all the bases
I told myself I did it to nourish
But nothing I touched would ever flourish

Garbage Day

If the next generation thinks clearly
And embraces truth, a huge pile of junk
Will go to the curb as they hold dearly
To what's right, knowing how to deal with bunk
Generations slowly sift, intertwine,
So it takes voices of reason to send
The message the emperor's crossed the line
Nude, the hole in his clothes too big to mend
It would be funny if it weren't so sad
Ultra-pretentious to change what's been right
For thousands of years, which means we've been had
Forever or just now seeing the light
Thinking clearly starts with seeing things straight
And not caving when someone calls it hate

Poem Before the New Year

It's windy, and I'm waiting on a cliff
For answers I can speak, not just perceive,
But even perception fails, not a whiff
Of explanation blows in to receive
I start to make things up, invent stories
That without absolutes, describe how it is
To have a life where the only glories
Are temporary, and taking a quiz
On reality is futile: your guess
Is as good as mine, so we all subscribe
Essentially to what we're taught; say yes
And stay within the boundaries of our tribe.
Meanwhile, I wonder what those three kings found
They passed here following a star around

War of Words

The conflict of our age deserves a name
The *War of Words* seems an apt description
Battle lines drawn as in an online game
No bandages or need for prescription
But gets more strident, aligned to their side
Convicting though convictions don't improve
Convinced but not convincing, much to hide
The truth notwithstanding, no one will move
The media has gone where the wind blows
The first casualty is truth in war
So journalism has sunk to new lows
There's nothing anyone will answer for
All just say what they want, with no holds barred
So far no sticks or stones, but we're all scarred

Grail

My travels in and around the saintly place
I'm pleased to say will be brought to life
In a new series, *The Holy Grail Race*
My co-producer is my lovely wife
Who found bones and simple tools that prove
The monkey predecessors of the pope
Evolved to hunting, eating on the move
And spread a crusade of life without soap
Nowhere is a sense they cared for clean
They just left garbage wherever they went
These habits then led to the magic bean
That grew and lifted them to what life meant
We found beanstalk traces that point straight up
And buried near the trunk, a giant's cup.

Politicanes

Name hurricanes after women and men
No more, rather a political cause:
Dorothy's Friends, rainbow-smoked from above, then
Hope it strengthens to *Force Six*, defies laws
Of nature and barrels into the coast
With a fury that roots out and destroys
All who go by gender. Grind them to toast.
Name another *E Climate Change* for joys
That will come when it plows through those who ask
What's the ideal global surface temp mean?
Ignore them! Don't answer! Take them to task
With a mammoth storm like they've never seen!
Feminists for Equal Rights to Abort
Could be next. We'll call it *Farrah* for short.

Against the Grain

Mat. 3:12, Isaiah 5:24

The generation ripens and is reaped.
I see and hear it coming close to me;
Soon we'll all be bundled, cast on the heap
Of history, verse twelve in Matthew Three.
We won't get one page: and what would you say
With not much time and space, and on deadline?
They landed on the moon one July day;
They boomed and busted, denied the Divine;
They didn't have a clue about the past,
Which led to their repeating old mistakes;
They made computer worlds that didn't last;
Between realities they chose the fakes.
Now the thresher's here to gather chaff.
We turn out to be burn outs. There's a laugh.

Tug of War

The rope was taut when I left to comb my hair
Thought nothing would change, someone save my place
And all be the same as when I was there
For a tug-of-war's slow and not a race
I never felt my presence had effect
I held the rope and pulled with all my might
But nothing budged, not that I could detect
So I thought I'd take a break for the night
But I extended my absence some years
Before I ventured back to the lagoon
Where I saw fruition of all my fears:
My half of the world was gone, way too soon
Now I wish I'd stayed put and pulled the rope
Better to give one's all and lose than grope

Commanders of the Law

Now that we have delegislated God
And have become commanders of the law
Strange to see our *witch hunts*, and very odd
Those who call themselves witches see a flaw;
They want respect, no one to use that term.
Soon a council of demons will demand
No horns nor pointed tails and be quite firm
On Halloween; vampires wanting a hand
As well, not just have full rights to drink blood
But open the blood banks so they can buy.
Meanwhile, fortune tellers claim that a flood
Of ghosts feel white sheets give them a black eye,
The wolf man wants exemption from his shots,
And Frankenstein his brain known for great thoughts.

Septic Tanking

Some things sink when you turn them upside down
Some flip back after being wrong a while
Do it to yourself but not the whole town
Armageddon's not *going out in style*
The church is shaped like an upside down ship
The world went wrong, so Noah built the ark
We don't sit in pews to give the Lord lip
The problem now's not knowing where to park
The flood is over but we're drowning now
We test the waters just to do a test
We flip things, push envelopes and say wow
And when the world goes septic, blame the rest
As the world tips now, one has to wonder
Will it flip back? I'm waiting for thunder.

Waiting Room

I'm in a waiting room, lost in a chair
Wanting to punch something since I can't fix
What's not broken, but can't come up for air.
I'm holding my breath and taking my licks,
I watch it all unfold in a tail end...
The conductor comes into the caboose,
Territory I'm ready to defend,
Asks for my ticket, and all hell breaks loose.
I want credit for the ground I've covered;
Well trained, my life's measured by ties and rails.
No one keeps track; it can't be recovered:
It's bouncing in me like a bunch of nails.
The whole journey's my stop, it's self-contained
The screeching halt's our route, waiting room chained.

The Medical Examiner

There was mileage on the body, no doubt
Callouses on hands and feet, lots of scars
Wrinkles, arthritis and clear signs of gout
No pristine organs for canopic jars
Perhaps this person would have lived longer,
The ME said, with less drinking, but some
Was good for the heart and made it stronger;
Without moderation, it tends to numb.
He'd eaten well and seemed to take good care
Of himself, but like his father, sat long
And walked little, lost most of his hair
Not saying there he did anything wrong.
There's just one thing that cannot be denied:
If he hadn't lived, he wouldn't have died.

What Matters

I worry my poems won't matter, but prayers
Mean more if you manage to bend God's ear,
And whatever poetry may do, where's
Its place on the list of all we hold dear?
No matter how much work one does to write
A good verse in hopes to move people's hearts,
Those souls will die someday without the light
Reflected but not contained in the arts.
Audiences drop away, they're replaced
By temporary beings so none last;
True understanding had better be based
On this fact, which unites us with the past.
Art should aim to wake each soul one by one
To what matters most before life is done

The Essential Creek

Somewhere as I touch the essential stream
There is a crossing-over point, a bridge
That bears me as I straddle life and dream
As if all truth were one point on a ridge.
I've seen it happen in a way most Zen:
A monk learns from a master a nice tale;
Even years later, hearing it again
It brings him back to where he must set sail.
Or put another way, why would it be
On any given day, that a truth still
Manages to fill real need? Because we
Find it's all from that same well on the hill.
So you'll hear strains of some lost tune you seek
As long as you're on the essential creek

Old Sayings

There are rains to wash the dirt from the air,
Sooner or later washing to the sea,
Falling as rain after they get there,
Making the world as clean as it can be.
But what will wash one's spirit of the muck
That builds up over a lifetime of sin?
Truth beads away like water off a duck
As we're resigned to facts we cannot win.
Given we will die, we just turn our back
On what promises to renew our soul.
We'd rather seize the day and hit the sack
Than believe there's a way we can be whole.
We even have a way to close the doors:
Take what comes and say, *When it rains, it pours!*

Strength Through Gear

I engineered strength into all the gear
I'd eventually wear when the time came,
So I could start my mission without fear
Quite protected for what was not a game.
There were trade offs, as in order to build
An armor to stand against what I'd face
One can't be both agile and not be killed.
I designed it to lead in the arms race,
Be years ahead or else be left behind
In smoking pieces on the battlefield.
I spent most of my life striving to find
What all seek: to be able not to yield.
My armor is ready, the time has come;
Too weak to lift it, I look very dumb

One Note Harmony

Sing me the real truth, a snippet's enough
As a wet finger on a crystal rim
Produces wind chime tone in one firm buff
Identifying in that single skim
A character that puts it above glass;
Or shards of a broken hologram
Still containing the whole, in smaller mass
Visible in a cursory exam.
A piece is all I need to be inspired,
As aroma can whet an appetite.
Please start the singing as I'm growing tired
Say the word, and I'll strengthen as to fight
I know the moon when I see just a line
And feel my sea pulled like my blood is brine

My Own Critique

Taking in a verse by a famous man
I felt highlights of spirit, then alone.
Is that all this can do, all it can?
I asked, not that I want to pick a bone.
But I wonder, is it like a day off
To sit and have this kind of truth applied?
What good does it do? Doesn't cure a cough...
As it's Art, who's to say whether it lied?
It doesn't matter. There are too many ways
One can either write or interpret things
Of this nature. Understanding decays
Though, when it allows that such garbage *sings*.
I suffer from a sense standards are set,
When they've gone as low as they can get

Judgment

My words packed in orders as on a stem
Seeds in the fruit; concealed in cadences
Then are reborn, squeezed from coal into gem
But while young, I did as the maiden says
   I went into the library stacks, made
Zen piles of books the same as flat beach rocks
Put them in order that would never fade
Rest the mind on each pile, and it unlocks
   In a dead universe there are faces
But no one can see them. Without a mind,
A great nothingness pervades vast spaces;
But if you're reading this, there's much to find
   I'm slowing down in everything that numbs,
   Readying to lie still when the day comes

The One Song

All the great music comes from a deep well
Where there's just one perfect song, hard to reach,
Where those who find it all say their song fell
Into their mind, something no one can teach.
In the beginning, there was just one song.
It touched everyone with a profound joy.
Others tried to imitate it; before long
There were lots of songs trying to employ
And reach the same place, but a step removed.
This brought anger, and some began to hate
The one song that continuously proved
The everything else was just second rate
So they buried it, but right there a spring
Burst since the one song, well, it had to sing!

Focussed Below

The whole universe can stand on its own,
But let me appoint myself to explain
Take a black part of the sky that's unknown
Magnify it, and new galaxies reign.
Somehow yet we look up and see some stars;
Most of the time just live during the day,
Wrapped up in buying houses and new cars,
Feeding our appetites in every way.
So the magnitude hardly works at all
To affect us by expanding the mind.
Ironically we're caught up in what's small
Focussed less on what's ahead than behind.
Above and beyond be damned. What's below
Is all we know and all we need to know.

Low Down

The trees might all have their standing orders:
Take root and be silent. For all we know,
Elephants mentally cross borders
And talk to God where we are blocked. Although
We acknowledge that birds can navigate
Great distances by an instinctive guide,
We don't feel we lack anything innate,
And what we don't understand we let slide...
We assume all nature is less informed
Than us, unconcerned with all that we miss,
How insect mind collectives work when swarmed;
Though dull, our closest analog's a kiss.
There's intuition we can't understand,
Dead to the world, thinking we're in command

Passive Voices

The world's on fire now, but it's not at war
The sky is red with blood though, which is smeared
In flaming waves that no one can ignore
There isn't a soul that hasn't been seared
I'm recalling better days decades past
The sky was dark, clear with many a star
But I've just realized this, and I'm aghast
It's only now just come up on radar:
All these years, the bonfire was being built
I can see trucks again; in the background
A flurry of action going full tilt
We never much noticed, nor heard a sound
But now it makes sense what was being done
We lit the match with pride there was no gun.

Recognizing Spirit

The imagined statement, perfectly wise
In point of fact does not exactly state
In points and facts, but also in their guise,
In poetic ways that articulate
What words cannot though only words are used.
So the highly enlightened state of mind
Needs words one at a time that aren't confused
To recreate concepts only divined
Until the highest understanding's shared
Whereupon all words can be put aside
Where there's no more inklings to be compared,
And nothing more that can ever divide.
But to recognize and then get near it
You'd already need to know this spirit

The Old Windmill

I'm an old windmill beginning to creak
Where I can be heard from a mile away.
To tear me down would take about a week
But as a fixture most want me to stay.
There's something about me, the way I turn,
My weathered look, my texture and my sound.
One pile, one match, and away I would burn,
And I'd be one less a scenic background
No, I know I'm something worth it to keep
Though some want my land for resource untapped,
Or to grow corn, or to raise cows or sheep.
It's *moulin* to *moo lawn* if I get scrapped
But while I'm here, all stop to look at me
And I never stop, as you can well see

Starting Through Woods

The hour closes in where I must begin
To bring some lifetime matters to an end.
I've nothing to lose but a lot to win,
And doing nothing's what I can't defend.
But it's a bit like having an old car
On blocks in the garage for many years;
I've tried to push it, but I don't get far,
And how to start it? Well, I have my fears:
How will it run? Will it stay on the road?
Will it carry my cargo where I want?
I'm the old car; I have keys but a load
To get rid of that continues to haunt.
Ok, I'm ready, but first I must sleep;
Miles to go, so I hope it will be deep.

Staying on the Line

Imagine an elusive paradigm
In subconscious orbit, sensed now and then,
That to never catch is a kind of crime
Considering it's always in your ken.
But almost as if designed to elude
It isolates your blind spots and lives there
That you sense only in a certain mood
But cannot coax out of its murky lair.
In time you give it a featureless face
And recognize its amorphous profile.
You let it fly; it's something you embrace
You come to think of it as having style.
Only later you see when it's too late
The hook's set quite deep where you took the bait

Saying Grace

Closing words on an ordinary night
After a long day and a bad headache
Having agonized at the country's plight
Surrounding the news all being quite fake.
The hyperbole is beyond belief
With actors and actresses telling lies.
Cooking burgers outside was a relief:
No one complained there were not any fries.
I trust the power I want to God's hands.
The best I can do is center the cheese.
I can't control the world or make demands
But share bread and wine with those on their knees
At a table where peace passes under-
Standing, which makes my enemies wonder.

Mine Tunnels

I dug the mine tunnels pretty far, deep
In the bedrock, and even went so far
To reach what I was looking for, to keep
While they argue about it in some bar
You cannot begin to deconstruct lies
Without learning properly how to think
A flawed ideology still relies
On true belief, so have another drink
Though your logic's a stacked deck hill of beans
Force your power: use your power with force
The ends you reach will justify the means
Truth be damned as long as you stay the course
Beside what I found there were bones like yours
Dead, defeated old dogmas, dinosaurs.
    10.31.18

Dead or Alive

When you sell your soul you get protection
Where when you break the rules, they don't apply
As hypocrite you won't face rejection
The godly are kept low while you fly high
Corrupt journalists look the other way
Ignore when you put your foot in your mouth
Others will burn for things less than you say
And you'll have a summer home in the south
But again, the price you pay is your soul
Betray the truth and get a life of ease
While young, it appears to be the right goal
But when you're old, you'll see it was just a tease
Then, while reviewing the damage you've done
Think of that withered soul the devil's won

I am the World

I am the world, not all you leftist fools
You're a desert wind, a blip on the screen
I'm the foam that comes back to shape, the pools
That refill when emptied, always serene
You call me hater, boiling with your lies
You twist the truth for power and control
In the end your ideology dies
Because quite honestly, it has no soul
You come and go like seasonal flu
Causing pain and discomfort, but we heal
At your worst, you kill more than a few
But there's no way you can win, that's the deal
Theory fits life like a body the cross
You fit the world's neck like an albatross

Down From the Heights

I am called to leave a message but don't
know what it is, to whom it should be sent
or why I was chosen. Over nearly
fifty years I've lived, I might have come to
know why me, what there is to say and to
whom. I never had it right, as when I
was called to leave this world, I couldn't bear
the thought that nothing of wonders I'd lived
was preserved in refuge for essences...
Then I despaired — and soon I recognized
the message was for me. It said, *You Fool,*
and then dropped me from the heights to open
as an orange bursts with all that's inside,
drawing a captive crowd of wasps and bees

Feeding Frenzy

I wanted to be in the mix, but tricks
In culture like big vultures swooping down
On dead meat, hung around and got their kicks
Picking at truth's carcass, rap came to town
A mishap, a load of crap by the bones
Of the noble beast that came to its end
Not like some sudden road bend where a car
Goes over a cliff, but silliness penned
And blasted, cast like last call at the bar
Juke box nuked, fluke in high falootin' tones
But only flesh goes extinct in the stink
Spirit still shines in a way that refines,
But the base response, as waterholes dry,
Is eat, drink, don't think, for instincts don't lie

Stick in the Mud

I turn all my thoughts to verse and broadcast
From a raft on a river full of mud
Which slows down what some people wish were fast
You'd say the sound my bell made was a thud
But basing it on their response alone
Rather than the quality of my thoughts
Is errant. Just because you hear some moan
And cover their ears means nothing. The dots
Before us will begin to grow in size
There are new ears ahead; some may listen
Word precedes us, and not all believe lies
Let's toast the raft we forgot to christen...
Good thing I brought a magnum, now a crowd
Of stick-in-the-muds like me wants it loud
    10.26.18

Safety Off

The trigger was a crescent moon, blood moon,
With two, three or four shots left to be fired
Hard to say since I stopped counting too soon
Fairly certain an assassin was hired.
I keep thinking of the crescent, it's strange
I never noticed such a thing before,
Now I'm blinded by its glint from downrange,
Which turns to a blind spot I can't ignore.
It grows and starts to take away my sight;
I look at the moon and just see a slice,
I see it slowly turn red; if I'm right
I'm being targeted, squeezed in a vise,
Feeling the full scope, its laser-dot tease
Joining the silencer shooting the breeze

The Baker

The baker had a way of giving me
crumbs when I was a boy. I would reach high,
try to put my hand on top of the glass,
as long as I couldn't reach, he'd feed me.
I learned to hold back as my arms grew long
to stoop in retaliation for my
increasing height that seemed to know no bounds
I covered myself with a bulky coat
to hide my crouch, but finally he saw
through the ruse and threw me out on the street
By the time that happened, I had grown up
and hadn't learned much beyond how to beg
Now he won't hire or feed me. I'm a crumb
the beasts of night stretch their paws to devour

Good Soldiers

My mind style needs to die because it's free
In a world of power, to control me
Has always proved to be impossible
So when the occasion comes, I must go
And all like me, unless perhaps we're armed
Even in some cases a whole nation
To combat that they must infiltrate it
Take away the ability to think
By taking over the schools, teach the youth
The ideas that go against being free
By breaking it all down to a big lie.
When the time comes to put away the free
Those who've been lied to will do it with glee
Good soldiers come from kindergarten, see?

The Buzz

Something about the world's never going back.
All this shouting, hitting closer to home,
All the voices, we're all under attack.
The truth isn't easy, you have to comb
The beachhead, separate water from blood.
So the social media, crowds on streets
Both virtual and real, dragged through the mud.
Moral codes going, going, gone, three sheets
To the wind. I used to sit in a chair
And read the paper, it seemed far away.
Something now seems to be choking for air
It's knocking on your door to make you pay.
The world's not coming back the way it was
The roar will get deafening is the buzz

Synching

I know the ingredients are the same,
But this is coming out different I know
There are many factors, but none to blame;
It isn't in the oven or the dough,
But there are like lights that flash on the street:
If you watch long enough, they're soon in synch,
Lighting at the same instant, exact beat,
Then back to random pattern in a blink.
There are moments of greater cogency
In those who have little and tiny wit
When things line up, perhaps it's only me,
But a true witness is less dull, more lit,
And science that explains streaks in the sky
Should inspire questions, not amputate *why*

Putting Others First

Now I'm hearing I don't put others first.
I'm halfway to the center of the earth
Digging a deep hole, the heat at its worst,
Which I've done like a midwife to give birth.
It's a deep shaft that aims straight for the heart
When finished I would give others the key.
On the surface, it simply looks like art
It's just a blueprint I let them all see
No one believes I'm really in the same hole
That cuts through rock a thousand miles and more.
Some understand how I've given my soul
To the effort of getting to the core.
But no one fathoms it's a lonely task
To do for others what they didn't ask
       10.22.18

Walking into Ether

Trying to describe this thing that comes close,
I work to be exact but still fall short.
Taking it at a distance, there's no dose,
And without any facts there's no report.
Still, I feel it's worth the effort to try.
Facial recognition in a cartoon sketch,
Like capturing the essence but a lie;
Depict the most noble man as a wretch,
I hope I'm touching on the theme at least.
Judging by what I've said, I've badly missed
Blindfolded and spun, I must pin the beast:
I thought I had a tale but won't insist,
Find I'm on a mission where I forget
The scope and purpose the closer I get

Awake and Unwoken

When evil's thrown into the deepest pit
And hits bottom where the pit is then sealed,
In order that nothing escape from it
All spirits outside the pit will be healed;
Then this slab of living, unwanted scum
Whose whole purpose is to bring on despair,
To take enlightenment and turn it numb,
Ineffective and unwilling to dare,
Will lie feeding on itself in the dark,
The place marked or not, off limits to all,
Not like some tomb on a walk in the park,
But a dark star in eternal free fall:
Trillion-legged beast, every knee broken;
A nightmare both awake and unwoken

101

Future Tense

I remember the circle of dead grass
Where my father built the pool each year;
We remember the yellow chlorine gas
And the masks they rushed to put on in fear.
I recall the lead tire weights we would melt
To make soldiers we'd crack out of each mold;
We recall bullets flying while men knelt
In trench mud wondering if they'd grow old.
I carved my initials into a tree;
They carved theirs on a cold cave wall in France
Feeling the rumbles of artillery,
Each bright circle flashing someone's last chance.
I'd make fast currents in the pool and turn
To face the force, the dead grass soon to burn.

A Claim

These are the times I lived; these were my years.
First I thought the world perfect; now its sins
Occupy me; it's all anyone hears,
It's all a fight to win that no one wins.
All I really want is to understand,
Not get enamored with anyone's views,
All the talking heads talking on demand:
At the end of the day there's no good news.
Then my thoughts go back to that little boy
Who saw the good, knew nothing about death,
And my faith tells me beyond this there's joy
That makes it worth breathing to the last breath.
My slice is no different; it's all the same.
Find where the real truth lies and stake your claim

Turning off the News

I turned the news off, not wanting to hear
The incessant craziness of mankind.
Even the use of that term, it's made clear,
Is unacceptable to Godless mind.
There came a point I had to walk away,
Seek silence to bring my thoughts back to peace,
Reweave my spirit that started to fray,
Turn the frantic build up into release.
I didn't have to hide like a snowflake
In some dark corner where I wouldn't melt,
But open at center and try to wake,
Find the light before which sages have knelt.
Sooner or later we each have to choose
The right path or burn in the caustic views

Sheltered Lives

We donned the teletype tapestry shroud
When it was spitting white, clunking out news
Of man making it to the moon, the cloud
Of an iron curtain shadowed our views
But could we go back and unwind the scroll
As we slept in church and in Sunday school
We'd soon find the glowing atomic hole
And then unwrap back to that bloody duel
The white sheet tucking us in as a boom
Of babies starts fresh on its own new tract
Mindful of war in an idyllic room
Of toys blessed to keep them safe from the fact
Now we race to unfold it to reveal
What's being cut out of the fake newsreel

The One Thing That Fits

Perhaps I may salvage this after all,
Picking up enough pieces of the age
As it was before the shattering fall,
Bring it back to life on a single page.
To at least get a pulse would be my goal,
Then give it time to get back on its feet;
The idea's to give the world back its soul,
Which it lost like a *Musical Chairs* seat
Through usurpation, locked out of the game;
But the power grab leaves the rest for dead.
Then comes craving truth; starvation's the name:
Torso on its knees flailing for its head;
Then it tries on everything it can find,
But there's just one that fits: its right mind.

Inching During Blinks

At the end of the great freedom, he died
Without detecting encroaching control.
The transition was slow, it did not glide
Into view but inched during blinks, its goal
The total supplanting of the free state
Without any force but by slow degrees,
Little by little until it's too late
Like warmth overtaken by a long freeze.
Then without any judgment or fanfare
They buried him the same way it was done
In his own time since his people were there,
Sowing last religion where there'd be none,
Then walked off not knowing how much was lost:
Right back into another holocaust

Truffle

I saw a truffle and thought of my brain
Shrunken and buried in the forest dirt
But wanted by some enough that they'd train
Dogs and pigs to sniff it out like dessert.
So shrink my brain down to a concentrate;
Get all of its essence into a spoon...
How much should you add to make your stew great?
What would I contribute to a baked loon?
You cannot help but want me in your dish,
The greatest chefs have reservations though;
They come to turn up noses, say they wish
To hurl, but secretly are eating crow.
All my life my brain was just some bland rice;
Now a little goes a long way as spice.

Kudzu Crossroads

I came to a crossroads and left a note,
A long-winded rant on all that I felt;
Others who arrived there might wish to quote
My words, and a few hearts might want to melt.
So I wrote them and chiseled them in stone
And looked and thought it made a decent base.
It needed a statue: me on a phone
Calling the whole world to speak face to face
And pointing the right way to go from there,
Which could be adjusted if I were wrong.
But at just that moment a thoroughfare
Opened; the crossroads gone before long.
The metal and stone I've put up for sale
Lie buried in dense woods on a lost trail

Only This

Only what I saw, only what I heard,
Only what I did, only what I said,
Brains thousands of times smaller than a bird
Know more in instinct than all I have read.
Only what I taste, only what I smell,
Only what I think, only what I feel,
Knowledge of good and evil leads to Hell,
The devil wants your soul, you make the deal.
Only what I want, only what I sense,
Only what I seek, only what I find,
I've packed in so much life, why am I dense
With so much time, so little peace of mind?
A creature that its own self can deceive
Measured by faith in what's right to believe.

The Devil's Handbook

The devil's handbook fell into my lap,
And I thought I'd look before he'd be back,
But it struck me he took me for a sap
And was taking a deliberate crack
At getting me damned somehow for the book.
Though I don't think myself an easy mark,
And also all I did was take a look
When it's a long volume, and it was dark;
I didn't pick up much I didn't know
Already, but I'll try to summarize:
The plan of evil mutates to what's so
Important to us in the shape of lies.
He never claimed the book; I said it's mine
Critics call it inspiration divine

106

Underlying Code

Imagine the heralds are archers, horns
Full of arrows, each note is a blow dart,
And the musical message you'd hope warns
Everyone instead goes right through the heart;
But not in any way that quickly kills.
These tones have a deep underlying code
They spell it out clearly so that it fills
The mind with revelation like a load
Is lifted; enlightened, one is then free,
But at the cost of dying in the same
Timeframe as it were, somewhat musically
With justice spelled out, so one takes the blame.
The process can take decades to unfold,
Darts sticking out we'll understand when old.

Selling the Cellar

I'm just an old basement filled to the brim;
A musty cellar, which describes my brain,
Held together by an essence of whim
Though heightened at times, generally sane.
All I contain from my life is a base
And basis for my views to an extent;
There's far more than memory, it's a case
Of an inner mix that starts to ferment.
It's a process that makes one something new,
Which can also become a disaster
Spirits are made more than born; if that's true
It boils down to, *Who is your master?*
The ruling thought determines if one's free
And what there is upstairs for all to see

Totem Tale

The angry tiki face becomes a mask
First as pareidolia, then in a dream,
Finally into wood, inspired task
To scare the whole tribe to become a team.
The masks become the center of a dance;
Even fire by comparison seems tame.
Plant extracts become paint, or induce trance
That calls evil from realms the men can't name.
We'd think the mask is bonding to the skin
When in fact it's the other way around:
The wood becomes infused from spirit in
The dancer, who's turned empty and earthbound
As demons take the soul to distant realms,
And those left carve new faces from the elms.

Wisdom Blockade

The central issues were neutral. They spawned
Opinions, which we were free to debate.
The question, *What do you think?* was what dawned
On me, remembering. But now there's hate
For those who won't think along the same lines
As teachers, who take the catalyst out;
And rewards for thinking have turned to fines,
Humiliation: the louder they shout
The more they believe they're right in their cause.
The more silent the opposition means
They've won arguments, can lay down new laws
Though it won't add up to a hill of beans.
Wisdom's emergent, a kind of gestalt
A long journey some are trying to halt

Baby Bust

The slow winding down of the Baby Boom
Now in another *seventies* of stall;
The first was the decade, when I assume
It ended; now we're reaching that age: all
Of us now in the last chapters, tail ends
Like sooty embers of a huge firework
Trickling down and starting to wear *Depends*,
Natural process toward going berserk.
We resisted everything we were taught
And fulfilled some great myths, made them come true;
We accepted science, left God and got
What we deserved for all we didn't do:
The post-war generation of spoiled brats
Now worse than red-tape loving bureaucrats

No Middle Ground

You take what you call the so-called high road,
Go to great lengths to say it's not so high;
That I brought it down with my heavy load,
But you'll build it back up or at least try.
Meanwhile you relegate me to the low
Regions where the roads are in disrepair.
My *high-road* methods will improve it so
The day will come you'll want to go back there;
And sure enough the high road falls apart:
You had no plan, tools or spirit to give.
Now you shout me down, call me an upstart
And push me off low-road lands where I live.
Soon both roads are awful, and we both die
With no God, you descend; I take the sky

109

Chicagoland

This is a part of earth without earthquakes
No volcanos or pyroclastic flow,
No rockslides or tidal waves, for lands sakes,
No glaciers or rivers of mud that go
Barreling along full of old dead trees,
No seasonal monsoons or desert heat,
No droughts or sandstorms or those killer bees,
No hurricanes or Ebola to beat;
But do not worry, we have our full share
Of murder and theft, putting God dead last,
Bearing false witness, adultery's not rare,
Keeping the Sabbath's a thing of the past,
Dishonoring parents, coveting all...
The land seems stable, but we're in free fall.

Magnification

I wish that I could photograph a thought
And then enlarge it fifty thousand times,
Imagine the finest details you sought
Coming to light like small patterns on limes.
The intricacies have no boundaries there;
It's we who can't see beyond what we can.
Yet we're fascinated by strands of hair
Or fruit flies in a molecular scan.
But somehow we can't get a closer look
At the shape of ideas or space they fill;
Fibers inked by a letter in a book
Magnify, but not the desire to kill
Imagine thoughts under a microscope;
I'd like to see an expansion of hope.

Something With God

Here's something with God, a human being,
So they throw him in jail, put him away,
But it doesn't stop people from seeing
Good and repeating what he used to say.
Here's something else, a book about the Lord
They ban its publication and arrest
Anyone caught reading it, put the sword
To the neck but not the book to the test.
It turns out the book contains all His words
And promises, prophesies, truths and more.
It's been burned and banished, thrown to the birds
Yet it's here, intact, touching to the core.
Where God's in lemon, they'll ban lemonade
Yet all will want a taste: that's how it's made

Test Pool

There really should be a kind of test pool
To dip things to see if they pass muster.
Too much is just accepted as a rule;
Dullness too often passes for luster.
Think if you will of Achilles' mother
Giving her son a blessed second dip
As his heel showed weakness, so another
Plunge into the first pool with a good grip
On the strong heel, and then Troy would have won.
It's not like simply *for want of a nail*,
But more about what's daily said and done,
As we put our faith in what's doomed to fail.
There is such a place to test the spirit:
False power keepers don't want you near it.

111

The More Outcast

While I stood being infused with the light
A steady beam aimed at my heart and mind,
Darkness dwellers rose, bristling at the sight,
And put to use whatever they could find
To block the streaming light and knock me down.
To some degree, they managed to succeed,
But in those days there were many in town
Who withstood undermining of the creed
And made sure the light continued to flow.
I wonder had I received a full dose
What I'd be by now and what I would know,
Much improved without getting grandiose,
Less besieged and mortified by the past,
But the more enlightened, the more outcast

Odyssey for Shut-ins

The great voyage of home and coming home
My basement is Circe's island, the years
Passed there are lost to me; and then the dome
Of the utility room, is where beers
Are stacked from brewing for the cyclops beast,
Polyphemus, Poseidon's son, now blind.
I did his laundry there, soap next to yeast
By my private cabin, where I work my mind.
From there, I plan escape to the upstairs,
Through sirens, Scylla, Charybdis, ahead;
How to manage passing through these three lairs
Through the living room, the kitchen, and bed,
The decades have passed on this ship I sail;
To reach my true home in God I won't fail.

The Fix

To not just *get it*, but to get it right
Might sound a whole lot like just splitting hairs,
You join one of many sides in a fight
Where the world's a brawl, and nobody cares
About the real truth since for each what's true
Is where they stand, which they defend with zeal.
No one considers it as just a view;
Everyone equates truth with how they feel.
Most of the time, once someone really gets
An idea, there's no effort to compare
And understand other views. No one vets
Their position for truth, which is unfair.
What is right is out there, somewhere in the mix;
Line it up with clues in you for the fix.

Safe Harbor

The sonnet gives you all the room you need
To open, explore, study and complete
A topic or express a feeling. Freed
From being vaguely sensed, it's quite a feat
To reveal what would otherwise be lost,
Significant emotion so to speak,
Which once clarified makes it worth the cost
Yet remains something one should want to seek;
For the approach strips the same mud away
That we all wear before we reach the shore,
Like ships near a sandbar catch ocean spray.
But it's the clear light they seek, and what's more
It warns, directs, reminds or serves to please;
The sonnet's a bright lighthouse near rough seas.

To Bring You Home

Searching for perfect thoughts to bring you home,
Something to fully grasp, forever hold,
Infinite yet contained in this small poem,
Open flat to bring you into the fold;
It's always on my mind, which is a net
Cast into vast surroundings here inside
Though what I'm looking for I've not found yet,
I feel just might float in on the next tide.
So I keep waiting, scanning every wave
Almost like watching for you to appear,
Learning as I do it how to be brave
No perfect thought nor signal that you're here.
It's lonely but for God and every star
That fill me with a sense that you're not far

Oversight

Why do they need to oversee the way
I think, when in the end, just love and peace
Are my true goals? Why control what I say
And do, when the free state was the same grease
That delivered them to where now they seem
Intent on carrying out their sole will
Which is neither love nor peace? There's no gleam
Of hope if you swallow their bitter pill;
It's all about their having the control,
Something you started with but soon will lose.
You won't be asked again, you've sold your soul
In the first vote and lost the right to choose.
By your thinking, selecting them to rule,
They'll oversee life like you're some old fool.

Whistle While You Can

Do you think that something's changed and we're done
With millions dying at a time whether
Due to class, race, religion, war or none
Of the above as in plague or terror?
A calm settles over the wasteland caves,
A truce perhaps after so much mayhem
To resurrect our motto, *Jesus Saves,*
Knowing the root from which all good must stem,
We may not know the future but can judge
From the past, and not feel blindly secure.
We slide to chaos refusing to budge,
Take our chances letting it be the cure.
The next great wave of death is likely soon
So whistle while you can a lovely tune.

Out of Whack

Imagine hot, off on its own, saying
It's not going to cut through cold anymore
Then cold blasting we'd better start praying...
When it relaxes its freeze, we're done for.
Imagine when light says it's had enough,
And will go so far to turn off the stars,
While darkness maintains its murk's all a bluff,
Which will be brought to light in its memoirs.
Then deep and shallow and other extremes
Like boy and girl, and also high and low
Weigh in as well, for they too have their dreams:
Go wanting to stop; *stop* wanting to go,
But they never get so out of control
In a right/wrong properly-aligned soul

115

Deaf to the Spirit

What kind of words are these that just sound nice
Of wild swans near distant hills on a lake?
A watercolor, who'd look at it twice
When out the window's the same, give or take?
But for the ears of city students told
The poem is of the highest order, lines
Like these seem like music fresh and bold,
Where one or two dark clouds appear as signs
In the heavens, warning us what's to come.
But now I think perhaps there will be rain,
I guess also a flood along with some
Landslides that will wash out both tracks and train.
At the end of class, we walked down the hall
Still deaf to the spirit trying to call.

Inner Life

My mind's a yapping rain forest of noise;
Each book I've read imparts a butterfly,
Or bird, to a whole with balance and poise:
A world I will carry until I die.
But now, none of these books is being shared;
They sit closed on the shelves, gathering dust.
Teachers won't even explain why they've dared
Change subject matter, only that they must
Update imagined gardens from old toads.
So all that life stays pressed between the leaves
While the new politics makes its inroads.
Rain forests disappear, but no one grieves
A whole new order's buzzing in dead trees
Pouncing on the old one like killer bees.

Inspirational

A strong sense to create from viewing art,
Soon I feel filled with symmetries of mind
Where something's beyond what I know in part,
Somewhat delivered yet out there to find,
Strange like sometimes wind can act as a comb
Where fields don't look chaotic but ordered,
Somewhere you've never been that feels like home,
Gaining lands not known to have been bordered,
Or finding a shipwreck that's your lifeboat
That knows the way to treasures of the soul,
A buoy not on the surface as a float,
More marker of the depths of being whole,
The spirit of an aura passed along
That inspires poem or painting or a song.

Cuckoo

We were once so quick to let take truth's place
A kind of form of it, that filled a void,
Or rather got there first and won the race.
Almost like birds that watched their chicks destroyed,
Another species made it to our nest
And laid an egg near those we warmed to hatch.
The invading chick was not a good guest
Pushing out our young. The last of the batch,
We raised it as our own, this ugly breed
Larger and unlike us in every way,
It finally left us, learning only greed
And looked to do the same without delay.
You laugh and think it won't happen to you
Glad to find a third egg where you had two.

Captain's Chair

The mill is where my old loves try to call,
But the wheel squeaks so loud, in gulps not sips
That soon my old loves can't hear me at all.
They might prefer the roar and not the drips
Where I stand: there's a sea beneath they would love,
Subtle fragrances and intricate sounds,
But they've chosen water falling above
And romanticize our old battlegrounds,
Put an old mill on a quilt to cover,
Rather than take out stitches, let it heal.
These old gals don't so much want a lover
As one to keep their ship on even keel.
Captains in home chair cushions long to sail,
But the closest they get's to check the mail.

The Time for Fear

Have no fear, if you think God's dead, while you
Are in the peak of fitness and so young;
Have no fear since the reaper's not in view
And says nothing like he's missing a tongue:
He's not so fearsome when he's far away.
Have no fear as he seldom makes his rounds
Near you, and doesn't seem to want to stay;
Have no fear, it's not as bad as it sounds:
They take the dead away, it's not your turn.
Have no fear, if time were cash, you'd be rich;
We scare the children telling them they'll burn.
Have no fear, death's no hag or wicked witch;
Have confidence, don't let it fade
But when your time comes, be very afraid

Colors of Guilt

My project today is a patchwork quilt
Homage to mankind, taking from the past.
Essentially I wish to project guilt
With Stars of David for those who were gassed.
This sets the background to a starry sky,
Nooses not lassos for those who were lynched.
Will stitch it together in deep blood red;
Who sees this will not sleep well, that is cinched.
I'm calling it, *The Dreamland of the Dead.*
Who will be a critic? Who won't ask why?
It drapes our coffin when we sleep our last;
The stars above are now, but these aren't past
Please feel free to touch. It's that kind of quilt:
What's on our hands imparts colors of guilt.

King of the Bees

I stuck my hand deep into a bee hive
But was extremely careful not to move,
Became a part of it to stay alive.
As a result, science used me to prove
That man is in control of everything,
But people went too far when they declared,
(Science acquiescing) that I was King
Of the Bees, and built me a throne, six-staired.
Scientists filmed it, in case I got stung;
Everyone watched and waited in the hope
To see some disaster where I'd be flung
From my throne, covered with stings, a dead pope;
But I became what they couldn't explain,
Which is what drives modern science insane.

119

Tanking

Squadrons of fools, a generation wide,
Turned the skies dark but forgot about fuel;
They flew one first and last mission and died,
Except for one man, who watched and kept cool.
He saw it happen, but no one to tell
Made life tough for the man as he went home
In the flaming aftermath that was hell.
The wasteland was all his, and the sea foam,
But what could he do? He was all alone.
Then he was tapped and snapped out of the dream,
His mind had wandered to a *Twilight Zone*
Where though the world had died, he didn't scream.
Now as fools scorched earth, he felt he must fly
But ran out of fuel in an empty sky.

Marring What's Well

There's always something we need to fix;
Even a perfect system has its flaw,
But when marring what's well gets in the mix,
Striving to do better can kill good law.
When Utopia begins to replace
Imperfect systems that are working well,
It builds a prison wall and on its face
Paints a heaven in order to hide hell.
As we do our best, there are problems, sure,
But turning it all upside side will fail.
A *perfect* government will not endure
If its largest institution is jail.
Because it's life, there's much we must accept,
Not hold faith back from ever having leapt.

Asked and Answered

Embrace the truth, but first find what it is;
Don't just take pretty constructs passed along
Others won't let go of. Here is a quiz:
One: Between life and truth, which one is long?
Truth goes from alpha to omega. Two:
Given love and truth, which one would you choose?
Why choose? Given both, here is what to do:
Live them both to the hilt, and you can't lose.
Three: Why is truth the most important thing,
And why can't the world find it and agree?
Well, since some things may have a certain ring
And may get consecrated as if key,
We soon embrace what we cannot defend
And make real truth harder to comprehend.

Imprism

Why do we let those people run the show
Which they do so badly, taking power?
Disturb the status quo is all they know;
To ruin lifetimes takes about an hour:
Just get the teachers, give them common core,
Put fear in people to say what they think,
And rivers flow in new banks; what is more,
You must pretend it doesn't have new stink...
The rainbow too is often passed around
To clarify exactly where one stands:
You want things equal, don't you? That's the sound
Of rainbow bands trying to tie your hands.
Stay clear inside, above clouds as it were;
Smoke and mirrors work better in a blur.

Erasing Givens

Without God, man reverts to mongrel state
The calling to be pure lost on deaf ears
The first clear traits are an increase in hate
A rise in diatribe that preys on fears,
And ignorance, the self-affirming kind
That acts as if it's wise and has achieved
Enlightenment; an intolerant mind
Though, without any faith, having believed
Only in what cause fits to get ahead,
Improve one's status, by using the past
As scarecrow, and vilifying the dead:
Change social order on a scale that's vast.
To dismantle ancient truths, they're driven
To erase what's always been a given

The Sixties

The fuzzy figures all came out in droves
For the protest. At least now they are clear,
But how they came to be our treasure trove
Is not, and still is fading year by year.
The song writers, hardest to understand,
Are easiest to explain as abstruse:
Marbles in the mouth was once in demand,
It sounded clear, now hard to reproduce.
The poets too stopped trying to make sense
And rather wrote along the same strange lines;
What we thought was profound, though, was pretense,
Stupid or desperate, we thought these were signs
But made no sense: fuzzy was just a phase;
It all comes clear now through the purple haze

Rolling Heads

To build a waterfall, you need a source;
You can't just do it anywhere you'd like.
A river through the woods is nice, of course,
And watch for drop-off rapids as you hike.
Any natural ramp can be cut back
To make the necessary steep drop down,
Then you'll have the falls with a loud soundtrack
In a picturesque scene of great renown.
Next then you'll need a parking lot and gate,
Paved pathways with raised railing, to assist
As well as guide visitors, keep them straight
As police guards scan for those who resist.
Take those who won't comply for the long drop
Below we'll watch their heads roll off the top

Room and Board

The age I live in talks of being free,
But cameras issue tickets on the roads;
Around the world a social-credit spree
Rates citizens, as much as that forebodes:
Do as you're told, and you will earn the right
To work and travel, opposite for those
Who deny the system's power and fight;
The same as ever, they're fed to the crows.
As for my world, there's just too much in place
Like college homework, life's the DMV
With lines, so all is fair, but it's so base,
All governments taint with bureaucracy.
Now there's talk of one great new world order:
Prison room and board for every boarder.

Eggs of the Beast

They say it might be time to curb the beast,
Which comes after years of giving it play;
The thing's been trained to go ahead and feast
But they'd rather it would nibble all day.
It takes a huge swath out with its sharp claws,
Which once were soft, and its limbs were so small.
As it wreaks havoc, we can see the flaws
Of policies that led to this and all;
But still we don't change how we operate,
Appointing counsel to do a study.
Meanwhile the beast seems to be taking fate
In its own hands: rivers turn muddy
It spawns a sea of eggs in the waters,
One each to replace our sons and daughters.

Sounding Distant Drums

I feel pigeonholed in a dying art
That might be dead except a few of us
Still believe in what goes on in the heart,
Neglect of which forms spiritual pus
On society at large, infections
Resulting from deficiencies, severe
Lack of knowing right from wrong directions.
No moral compass of an inner ear
Pressing to the tracks to have an insight,
An educated guess to save the tribe
In preparation for the ultimate fight,
Which really does boil down to just a vibe.
But this is where true legislation comes
Unacknowledged but sounding distant drums

Sins of the Father

Father Laocoon, a priest with two sons,
Had married an accountant, bore him twins
But died, leaving him with only the nuns.
He joined the clergy and covered his sins,
But the church never quite accepted him
And looked for ways to push him out the door.
They learned about his marriage, took a dim
View of his having sons, could not ignore
Those facts and cut him loose one fateful day.
From that point on, the paperwork became
A beast that seemed called up to make him pay
In a nightmare with only him to blame.
His sons tried to help, but bills and late fees
Strangled all three of them, down on their knees.

The Proud and Ignorant

How quickly the sun could burn us to dust
Or cold space freeze us into a hard block;
We exist between extremes where we must
Toe a fine line in order to just walk.
But it's all provided here on a sphere
That suits us and gives us all that we need;
But some sharpened sticks and claimed they were *here*,
Looked at you as another mouth to feed
But will if you swear allegiance to them.
You can't just wander picking fruit from trees
The valleys are all owned, each stone and gem:
Should you find one, present it from your knees...
The hot sun beats down, and cold outer space
Surrounds the proud, ignorant human race.

125

July 2018

Sometimes we lose sight of obvious things;
When I was young, no matter who we were,
We were Americans. There were no kings,
Just a sense the greatest things would endure
Like freedom and liberty. Our values
Are based in the Ten Commandments, God's Law,
Which was engrained both in personal views
And in being American, no flaw
In the logic, and the proof was right there
In the person, family and the town.
Now they're trying to say none of it's fair,
Needs to be rebuilt as if broken down;
Of course it's a lie to distract from fact
Nothing is broken; it's just being hacked.

Resemblance

The fangs of time are drooped with an abscess;
Time's joints too are paralyzed with bone loss.
There's a creaking over the tick tock, less
When the moaning covers that like thick sauce.
This monster's leaking out from every seam,
What used to be such a well-oiled machine.
Its moon-phase calendar worked like a dream,
Lunar then to lunacy now is seen:
The call's out that time's escaped from the home.
With no family, and nowhere to go,
We all just hunker down, wait in the dome,
Busy ourselves with learning how to sew.
Soon they're saying how much we look like him;
They have no picture, plus our eyes are dim.

Rooted

I've gone from being of an opinion
To being of a certain mind, for God
Created us all *In the Big Onion*
But expects each to grow out of the pod.
Was that *Beginning?* Sorry, my mother
Told me about the big onion, that we
All came from one bulb, and then another
Grew to call us forth. But if we could see,
If we'd heard God's Word, we'd know not to go,
Recognize the evil there was a lure,
That we're meant to take root ourselves and grow,
Not be harvested, forget who we were;
And though I see the factories are full
They can't take me as hard as they can pull.

An Untold Tale of Ulysses

Found on Homer's floor, this omitted clip
From *The Odyssey*, translated for you:
It details how he's working on his ship
With his men after leaving Troy, when who
Should appear but Aeneas in his boat.
Now they have to answer, *Is the war done?*
Here are two sworn enemies, both afloat,
But each a remnant like nobody won;
One's trying to get home, and the other
Is off in hope of starting again.
Now they're here, with good reason to smother;
Each other, face to face with all their men.
With much to do, they just ignore, pass
And go their separate ways, both out of gas.

Books

Don't let good ideas lay dead in a book
And say that books have some power to save;
Why give the eyes credit for how they look
When you keep them closed up in a dark cave?
We know many books are great, true and wise,
But from the shelf they can't do much but wait
For readers to try those thoughts on for size;
And until they do, wisdom will come late
If at all, but those who write in that vein
Can only hope some care enough to learn:
That they will choose a route that's proven sane
And acquire understanding to discern.
Books help one reach higher under the feet
But once in mind there's reach that's more complete

Unstoppable Voice

I function as an unstoppable voice
But only on the off chance will you hear
Happening to pick this up, not by choice
But randomly flipping to this page here
Then I get shut up again, in the dark
Of wherever no one happens to be
Reading something else somewhere in the park
The last thing would likely be poetry
But it's a howling wind with soulful sound
The same size spirit that inhabits you
Blood salt levels like the sea, all around
It beckons, but one needs reminding too
Far from the waves, the small dose of these lines
Keeps you in mind of essential designs

Colossus Shard

I'm a small piece of a smashed colossus
That stood one foot on each side of the bay
Still above water as each ship crosses
I see two feet are all that's left today
My place was on the forehead way up high
Just above me, men watched from a crow's nest
They could see an invasion from the sky
But ankle explosives? They never guessed.
When they blew, the towering twins came down
The torso itself blew out such a wave
It rose up and blasted into the town
After that, there was nothing left to save
Strange to be a shard of what once was great
A remnant reminiscing past and fate

Testing the Spirits

If you're following anything I say,
Detect any vein of sense running though
That you'd consider making an assay,
Be sure to use the right tools if you do:
It's about how to measure clear thinking,
Which from any standpoint starts where you'd think
You do think clearly and without blinking
Dismiss what would otherwise make you blink.
So kindred spirits tend to gather round
The fires we build here for warmth and support,
Achieve community of spirit, bound
Only to truth, which is one island port.
You sail the world thinking it lives inside,
But look around and wonder when it died.

Stranglings

Finally, after a lifetime of work, drops
Of an essence form in their purest state
After all those years of what are called flops
This welcome emergence of what's first rate
But sadly, as wonderful as this seems
No one is here to care or show concern
The world appears to have abandoned dreams
Deciding there are better things to learn
Than truth as it is fashioned out of thought
As truth itself is being pushed aside
So children won't find out: they're being taught
The same dead ends that fail when they are tried
Each single brain can find truth and be free
But soon can't breathe in stranglings of the We

Abortion

I was a ball pitched at high speed and hit
Hard on the ground into the field toward short
I somehow managed to bound off a mitt
Into foul territory. In a sort
Of wild play that one doesn't often see,
I got lost against the wall, and the call
Was argued where nobody could agree
Until both benches emptied. Forget the ball!
The game was quickly called due to the dark,
But both teams filed protests and left the field.
It rained, and I got waterlogged. The park
Flooded. Decisions were made and appealed.
Finally they said the game must be replayed.
I never existed: what a charade!

Dance and Defeat

The world will defeat you, so have your day
Let it comfort you when you're in decline
Very few recall, but you had your say
And like everyone else, you crossed the line
You bought your trinkets and traveled abroad
You had your rich days after being poor
You blew it, felt like the worst kind of fraud
And lived through days of peace and nights of war
You made your moves and had death on the run
Your gambits were routine, death reeled you in
The band keeps playing, but your dance is done
Too bad death wages come from blinding sin
Life's a challenge, but you don't have a chance
Just memories of that day you got to dance

Ultimate Power

Ultimate power, quiet as the stars,
Lets the tiniest plant crack the sidewalk
Connects the moon and ocean, while it bars
Us through relativity, puts a block
On travel without losing time and place
For us, power is control, money, land;
Ultimately, life is brief; we must face
Losing all our power when the hourglass sand
Runs out, when we realize that we had none;
That it's ephemeral, even not real,
Yet in all ways consolidated, one
Force has it all, seems set to make us feel
Over a lifetime, to come to believe
A guiding hand has fingers in the weave

Line up the Dead

The future is known. It's the past that keeps changing.

First things first, get those dead people in line
How dare they not think as we do of them
Owning slaves, signing on the bottom line
Of documents of freedom, we condemn
This, and thus it's all tainted, so we must
Look further, to the war between the states
Those rebels held to what can't stand, we trust
You see their statues must fall, no debates
And no flag, we must purge our land of that
While we're at it, it's hurting some to see
Old Glory, and sports Indians fall flat
Trash all the dead have done to you and me
We do this for all who will come after
Also, purge that sound of sudden laughter

Jungle in a Design

The natural state is a thick jungle
When things are let go and not overseen;
The same goes for the mind, that we bungle
Into a chaos of thinking obscene.
So we tend the garden for higher yield,
And a flock with a shepherd is secure.
From afar you'll see the look in a field
That with man things aren't wild as they once were.
But cities reveal a jungle within;
In close quarters it all gets out of hand.
The preachers will tell you it's all from sin
That we're just sheep who are lost in this land.
By this we should see chaos in the night
But stars look tended, cared for in each light.

Distant Call

The hazy clouds make a ceiling at night
The moon's a kind of light fixture up there,
Though truth calls, in this world I have the right
To expect it to stay out of my hair.
But gray areas have a certain way
Of creeping up, taking over the place;
You learn to lie and be lied to, but say
The truth and you are all heart to heart, face
To face, though you've ignored its call for years.
Somehow you've come to define it in terms,
More like a freeze-dried version that nears
Water that flows away for fear of germs.
The clouds congregate, and still the truth calls,
Loud and clear even behind all the walls.

Shining Way

Can you not see Eden is possible,
Not from here forward, but that it was here?
It's like a bridge fallen, uncrossable,
But it once spanned a chasm and was near.
I look at trees and see people in love
In branches, twisting, forever embraced,
Spirits of an older time now above.
Our only clue to what they might have faced
Is they've no reason, no wish to return
As much in dark about us as we are.
Only we live now, with a chance to burn
It all down if we lose sight of the star.
Above Eden's closure, hidden by vines,
The bridge is long lost though the way still shines.

Fixing the World

The plan to fix the world cannot begin
Until you fix yourself, but hope in that
Fades considering you can't help but sin
And never can you get the world down pat.
Imagine standing, waiting for a cloud
To descend on a mountain, and you'll fight
It when it comes. Through thunder that is loud,
By light of lightning strikes, you'll make things right;
Those who get lost in clouds, the ones who lead
The world, make it appear that they have won,
But how can we trust any such great deed?
It's beyond us all when all's said and done.
It's hard enough work to make yourself right
Than expect to change others out of sight.

Complete Combustion of the Soul

In darkness, there are those who feed and grow
From the foulness that hides where there's no light,
Imagine a cave that's covered with snow
Cold inside and out, in eternal night.
But this place that can hold you is a weight
As well; when you're in it, it's on your chest,
So you're trapped, buried, a prison inmate.
But to the darkness, you're a welcome guest;
For those feeding and growing in the dark
Are nourishing a cold and deadly beast,
Numbed, not enabled; chained, not free, a stark
Contrast given they're alive but deceased.
And these *dead* fuel a furnace: chunks of coal
To ash: complete combustion of the soul

Knowing What Fits

In the deep lush of fluids and of flesh
As sensibility's subconscious folds
Into desire, life transforms two to mesh
As one, which initiates inner molds
With right parts of each to spark something new,
Like a tadpole in the warm swamp grows legs
To when a frog knows the place and on cue
Nestles instinctively into the dregs,
And without knowing, knows what to do.
So in cycles, spirit guiding in spurts,
Conscious yet driven mindless in the goo,
So much ecstasy that it almost hurts,
Life finds its way blindly with special eyes,
Knows what fits without trying things for size.

Knuckles Full

Knuckles full of scorpions gets to be
The status quo of deceit, let them go
And hell breaks open wide for all to see;
Chaos, once it gets going, seems to flow.
Handfuls of angry hornets are the price
One pays for telling lies, to release them
Is just another roll of loaded dice.
Your number's up defines the stratagem,
A bushel of snakes secured to each arm
Is a balancing act that must collapse.
It launches at others, who come to harm,
Without truth, it's just one of many traps.
The wicked here stand also to be hurt
But watch out for those with hearts full of dirt

Born in the Stream

Born in the stream I stood up walking fast
And strode to the shore starting a landslide
Carrying me to a mountain at last,
Which started an avalanche I still ride.
It's a buckin' bronco of a white cloud
On which I balance, surfer in the pipe;
To pop too soon would wrap me in death's shroud.
But I don't feel danger despite the hype
And have dreams of black sand on a long beach
Where I watch waves under a sky of stars.
I understand this vision's out of reach
But it sure soothes a psyche full of scars.
The snow never stops, it's an endless stream;
I was born to glide right into that dream.

Down to Size

If you take one picture to the other side,
And it's your whole life pressed onto a page,
The center will be you before you died
Like a lion that never knew a cage.
The rest must go away to be complete,
More would be like getting knocked on the head,
Waking in Elysian Fields of wheat
With partial amnesia, still being dead.
The photo chooses you to jog the mind
Post hypnotic suggestion of a sort
What single vital image could one find
To restore half swamp to a bustling port?
Any one of a kid, stars in the eyes
Should work, before the world came down to size.

Cue Sad Sax

The real cat wasn't so cool, but the cat
That plays him is. Yes, he plays him real cool.
There wasn't background music either that
The movie has. A silent life as a rule
Was all he knew, but with that big band sound
And jazzy saxophone filling the cracks.
The story in the movie gets around
Facts, gives him a girlfriend: a film that lacks
Sex appeal gets bad critical reviews
That kill it in the first week. What it needs
Is declaration that it's all big news
A sensation filled with glorious deeds.
Meanwhile, a flower pile on his grave grows
Where the cool cat himself kneels for a pose.

The Stain of Thought

If I wanted to come to my senses
If that were the goal, I'd think it would show;
Works are actions, inner walls are fences:
When you come to your senses, others know.
If you want to wake up, start with what's right,
And by stages, work up to save your mind.
The soul saving stage, people seeing light,
Feels last, but the light's always here to find.
Why would one not want to give it a chance?
The benefits, ends in themselves, don't end,
But to do nothing but stay in life's dance
Is to spin, not cycle up, but descend.
It's only within that one is bereft
But everywhere's the stain our thoughts have left.

Dropping off the World

It is said that checkout time is when
You've had enough of everything, and so
You take the whole world and all its men
And drop it off somewhere topped with a bow.
When you have given up and wish to leave,
You can make arrangements to disappear,
Putting it in a place where none will grieve:
Your planetary bowling bag, just gear,
To hide the world, leave all up in the air,
Just drop it off and remove your name tag
So no one will know you were ever there;
And that's it: do that, and it's in the bag
Never mind the thought you might leave a hole:
Crawling out of one is your only goal.

Blot

It comes not as a mad wish but a whim,
Full of yearning to unleash in a line,
A single flowing from an ink pen, slim
Clean and straight as well, which is a good sign
Of limits; there's no perfect circles here.
We're all stamped out in good time, just the same
As we broke the mold when born, make that clear,
Though soon we copied all except our name
And swore we didn't sell out or conform,
Fully sharing in the styles of the age,
Never released from all that is the norm,
Nor finding truth since it wasn't the rage.
Now wanting to spill it out, straight and true,
It blotches, and nobody has a clue.

Taken Alive

I like dead because it's cool, because there's
Nothing, is there? Just no more of life's crap,
That it all just drops away, no more cares,
And as they say in the business: it's a wrap.
Yes, I like dead because it's the true end,
Right? Just absolute silence, and no thought,
Nothing nagging like the loss of a friend;
None to say you didn't give all you got.
So I like dead well from that vantage point,
A deep and empty huge black hole, correct?
No new plane of existence to anoint
New consciousness, no soul to resurrect?
But much as at times it sounds good from here,
I'd rather be taken alive? We clear?

Paper Blizzard

Leaving the fragrance of our push like smoke,
Energy of our shape and of our force
As when the towers fell, it was no joke
That the forms lingered above their old source.
Lying in a heap, broken and in flames,
Slowly wafting down like an arctic snow,
Squeezing from clear skies the thousands of names
That no one remembers but all should know,
This is what we leave behind in the minds
Of those who knew us, our essence encased
In a loop carrying our soul one finds
Floating in mind away from all the waste;
In no small way, it tells them who they knew
As did the paper blizzard when it blew.

Snowing Crescents

It started snowing crescents in my dream
Amazing sight collecting everywhere.
It was an event so strange it would seem
Frightening, nothing like it to compare.
From behind, someone started to explain
How such a thing could happen, and it made
Me tired though I accepted it like rain
Or snow, something of the most common grade.
But why aren't rain and snow still amazing?
Where did we lose the child's sense of wonder?
To explain is a big step toward phasing
Out the visceral response to thunder
Just as we're used to the Big Bang theory:
Now slivers of truth fall, and we are weary.

Bottle's Eyes

As far as eyes can see in the bottle
Raised to our lips as we're casting our line,
Master of the craft, foot on the throttle,
The sunset is yours, the night is all mine.
Fish peck the star specks to a thousand lights,
Into a swirl that tells about the sky.
The Milky Way resonates with our rights,
Fulfilled somehow without needing to know why.
Whatever primal beast the waters hide,
Whatever lurks, we hope it takes our spoons.
We sense we have the upper hand, abide
By nature and at peace for many moons
But as the bottle drains, the one we've nursed
We troll toward shore, called back there by our thirst

Bean Stalking

Again I'm being asked to plow the field,
Which I will do when my office is clean.
But in a strange way, the contents are sealed,
No beanstalk here: this would have killed the bean.
No drought, my harp's where I can hear her sing,
But it's like I'm drugged; my body's on fire,
So the overgrowth in harvest won't bring
Anything anyway except a wife's ire.
I have a fee but say fie to my foe
Who fumes above in tempestuous clouds.
I keep the bean handy, I never know
When I might need it to escape the crowds.
And dispose of the giant, heaven's clown:
There's no room for both of us in that town.

Reason and Spirit

There's a point of over spicing, beyond
Which the stew's septic, one cannot eat it.
The same is true when the mix of all minds
Becomes so toxic truth won't defeat it;
Only the death of a generation:
Time cleans out the noxious tub as it drains
Mockers, scoffers with no veneration
For what's right, and any setbacks on gains
Can reverse themselves and again begin
To bring light to what became a dark age.
One voice is enough to shine light on sin.
One normal dying out to turn the page.
Meanwhile, that voice of reason and spirit
Is always there for those who will hear it.

A Swirling Presence

Youth is a swirling presence of good dreams,
But in major movements, it won't go far.
Slowly, in a normal process, what seems
Is replaced with what is, which is a bar
To great ideals, begins eroding hope,
And over decades while growing older,
The spirit loses grip, begins to grope
And tends to think the world's gotten colder.
Is one ripening or fading? The key
Is to embrace the inner life, cherish
The mysteries where to be blind's to see,
Where things eternal really don't perish.
Then age is fruition of youth's ideals,
You end where you begin, with all it reveals.

Arms and the Men

War is anger off the scale in the wealth
Of ability to trash talk with force.
Alone we sneak to the fridge, which is stealth;
With an army, you shoot without remorse,
Once a man commands thousands, when he moves
To scratch his nose, hundreds cross rivers south;
Waving his arm, tanks cross fields, which all proves
They're linked in every way from hand to mouth
So while you and I might yell at a dog,
His anger translates to a city siege,
A one-hour blitzkrieg that overruns Prague
A sneer's a barrage; a glare will besiege
State power loads you into its big gun
Where he points, shells will drop, and it is done.

The Big Lie

The peephole was really so very slim
Which is why diamonds were preferred throughput,
But now the hole is gaping, and the grim
Truth is the world sucks on its own big foot.
So now I can shovel through all I do;
No one waiting to measure or discern,
Each chair is now a broadcast station. Who
Is left to listen, wait until they learn?
But think of what's being taught at this point,
Hope's crawled back to hide in Pandora's box,
Thousands of years set aside, smoke a joint
And force tradition out, then change the locks.
Now the peephole looks out, tiny from jail
To one big lie the world salutes, *All Hail!*

How Are You Holding Up?

The Lord asks us to hold one another up
What's holding us up from that I wonder
Everyone just holds up an empty cup
Like holding the game up if there's thunder
But we're still being asked if we can hold
One another up in support of truth
But as truth goes, some are hot and some cold
The heart needs a brush up, gone after youth
The way it works, as to why it doesn't
Is we reach the point we hold up our rank
To drop one another down, which wasn't
Our intention, but have the world to thank
While holding friends up, demoted and robbed
Try to remember your heart when it throbbed

Farce to be Reckoned With

As the godless one took power, his hand
Went down, which gave a green light to a lost
Bunch who dream the world is at their command
But have no idea, concern for the cost.
But out they go, now free to learn to break
Laws with the excuse that the laws are bad.
Soon there are sanctuary cities, fake
Safe spaces where snowflakes keep cool, mad
That some don't buy into pushing aside
Thousands of years of faith and common sense.
But in the years since the godless one lied,
Though now there's an effort to mend the fence
And a believer who replaced the clown,
The evil circus still dances in town

Starting to Fade

Once you finish blooming, you start to fade;
You go through becoming, and then you go.
Once you make the grade, you start to degrade;
You make it, but passing it in the flow,
Reach the final chapters, then the last page.
You might even say it was all foretold,
To run out of all space in the space age
And go the only way where no man's bold...
So yes, in the end it's all about death,
That must cross your mind as air in the sky,
The very limits of your longest breath,
The oppressive silence when you ask why.
But stillness is known for what it instills:
A filter prospecting for what fulfills.

Canned

When you said you'd take the high road, I thought
I'd stay here, report from the marketplace.
You found the mountain spirit: while I bought
Trinkets; you breathed fresh air from God's own face.
Now you are reduced to some famous books,
Which the world received knowing how to read.
Meanwhile, I still meander by meat hooks,
Dangling fish and roasts, a whole mob to feed.
You know what the thunder said, what it means;
I only know the rumblings of a gut
Whose instincts amount to a hill of beans,
Collapsing when I climb back to this rut.
I wish like you to step off in God's hand,
But your route was fresh and true; mine is canned.

Quizzing the Test

Assume the senses cover all that can
Be seen, smelled, felt, detected and perceived
That there is no range of sound beyond man
That watching dogs react, they are deceived.
We know we miss a lot, but work within
Our limits fairly well. Still, what of those
Creatures that navigate (where to begin)
And the complex DNA of the rose?
Whole orders of sense not part of our gears
Found reason not to evolve, but our sex
Got pleasure in its realm, while sight got tears
While mixing them both gets you Oedipus Rex?
We're beings, and beings sense what is
But we only test for what's on the quiz.

Insulation

How can we insulate and keep air clear,
Keep the world believing it's all contained,
To feel no need to look further than here?
We were there, we can say, as we've been trained,
We are witness but witless to the facts,
We take the wrong side; it's the only one
We see, with numbers of contrary acts
So small they must lose, and we will have won.
So it is with an absolute control,
Especially the news is scripted lies;
The devil's happy to buy one huge soul
Easier than millions of little buys.
And so in ignorance we live and die,
Insulated so well we don't ask why

Right About the Rock

I sense design in murmurations, birds
Flocking and surging, amazing display;
Leave making calculations to the nerds
Though, and don't believe outright what they say.
In just a few weeks, we lost Billy Graham,
This age's quintessential man of God,
And Stephen Hawking, who denied *I Am*
Poster child of science, a little odd.
But like Graham, still at his work at the end,
Each explaining the meaning of all things
With their whole being, with minds that defend
An ultimate truth, but still two chess kings
Where one must win, not as murmurs the flock:
But because just one's right about the rock

Ankh

The sickly king, a cichlid in the mouth
Of Egypt, club foot, weak, wasting away
Is now a battle-hardened warrior
Based on a close study of his armor.
Now Tut races over the dunes, attacks
In his fine chariot, leading the way;
No longer the egg of cholesterol,
Now the yolk of strength within human shell.
So the mortal youth, brave as he is,
Goes down not in disgrace but in honor,
Though that kingdom is long gone from the earth,
The sands spit forth the dead fish, and it took
Scores of centuries digging in the dark
To reveal it's no minnow but a shark

Spirit to Spirit

Spirit to spirit, if we could do that,
Who would seek to open the chest that hides
All we work hard to keep under our hat,
Filled even with things that no one confides?
I want no barriers, least of all walls,
But the fact is that I live in a maze;
You'd get lost even in the straightest halls,
Which is the long route to my wicked ways.
The shortcut is to think you've touched my soul;
I leave it out there somewhere on the path...
Sense the connection, it's the only goal:
Complete yourself with someone, do the math.
I want to push the chest into the sea,
Sink it, but it drifts into eternity.

Day of the Dead

They celebrate the Day of the Dead here
And there's a skeleton's grin replacing
A child's happy face in ceramic gear
To remind us what we'll all be facing
But to me, it's the way the rocks are piled
Near the beach, formations catching my eye
One looks like a woman holding her child
Another appears to just be some guy
Sunbathing, and then I see it's just rocks
The waves keep pounding a thunderous roar
The sand's too hot, and everyone just talks
Selling, moving, or melts into the floor
I begin to feel the dead; they're lurking
But the rocks will tell you, death's not working

Climbing From the Pit

I want out of this world sometimes, I cry
For justice, seeing things that curl my hair,
So aghast that I can't even ask why:
The kind of evil where you sit and stare.
There are holes so deep sometimes in the soul
Where tears do not bring peace, and you can't stop.
Once you fall in, you cannot come back whole;
No bottom, and no longer any top,
But you find yourself somewhere in between
Deciding whether to live or just quit:
You'll never be the same from what you've seen
But growing up means climbing from the pit
Where just as you think what you see's what you get
Comes that feeling you ain't seen nothin' yet.

The Sun

A hand came out of the clouds to provide
In what were terrible times, and they took
What it offered gratefully. Aside
From food, they were also given a book
That would help them build within and without
So they did that, and for a time were great
Then wanted a bigger hand and handout
It was all about more meat on the plate
And as the hand grew, their hearts turned quite cold
They forgot the book, watched their culture fall
Where children wouldn't hear what elders told:
A diminishing place that once stood tall
Where a great hand of light turned fiery fist:
Desert sun that made it hard to exist

Quiet as Snow

As I watched my mother's tsunami wave
Roll through our lives uprooting everything,
I swore I'd tell the story and not cave
To fear of the kind of shame truth would bring.
As one watches homes being swept away,
There's a desperate sense while feeling helpless:
You know you can do nothing, but you say,
I'll get you for this, then deal with the mess
Left behind after the water recedes.
You find it leaves a wound that never heals:
Even decades later, the sore still bleeds;
Only those who've lived it know how it feels.
Same with my mother's wave, but I've let go:
And watch its fall as quietly as snow

149

Workers in Force

There's no shortage of the cruelest people
Ready to take over at new death camps,
To level the ground of every steeple
And scrutinize papers for proper stamps.
They're out there right now, waiting for the chance.
They're hard to spot, but they're easy to read.
They'll like to wave a gun to make you dance,
But they'll just as soon shoot as hear you plead.
If and when the day comes where they control,
And you happen to have known them before,
Watch as they treat you like you have no soul
Where they used to bring groceries to your door.
Those who would gas us are with us always
Where peaceful co-existence is a phase.

To Loralie

Stillborn July 18, 1996

The marriage is tied to the funeral scene
Ritual white veil as opposed to black
Hat shaped as a bell, with a tingle clean,
While the log sounds the gong with a strong whack
The procession of short steps; life is short
Stiff movement at the altar; death is stiff
Promises before a judge as in court
And candles giving everyone a whiff
To remind them of the ashes they face
It's all ashes to ashes and dust to dust
Flowers, rice substituting in this case
Mirrored image of the end without lust
A process to live, ritual to die
Release all the doves: they know where to fly
     July 18, 2017

Why the Grief?

Imagine a tree with billions of leaves
Where each one can fall at any time. The wind
Affects all at once, but some it just heaves
Off their branch while others remain quite pinned.
You and I both are leaves on this tree, draw
From it independent of each other,
But yet are connected by the same law
Of life, where every leaf is a brother.
I just figured it out as I shimmer
On my branch in a pleasant summer breeze:
We each start green, then our days grow dimmer
We turn yellow, curl, then float down with ease
We become the earth that feeds each new leaf
From branch to root, we cycle. Why the grief?

Releasing the World

The old man recalled when he was a boy
But was more interested in the change
That took place over years that brought him joy
In understanding, peace in the exchange
Where he was quite content to finally know
Things that he couldn't convey to a youth
Or to the whole world for that matter, though
It made sense to pull together the truth
As he saw it as some might benefit:
There's a tipping point for an open ear
That's emptying its wax. It hears the bit
It shut out, avoided year after year.
So the old man wrote a quick simple line:
Release the world and reach for the divine.

Gift of a Cloud

I was gifted by God of a great cloud
That He sent to completely cover me;
It surrounded and muffled what was loud,
Made sounds like hummingbird or hover bee.
I used to live in a world of clear sky;
I knew what each day would bring, what I'd do,
Which was what I always did, asking why,
As if I got red that should have been blue.
So this cloud fogged the whole picture. I saw
Nothing anymore like the way it was,
Forced into having to live by the law
And face the music, a kind of strange buzz.
Such a cloud is unusual and rare;
I soon understood it answered my prayer.

Rage of the Blind

There's a state of belligerence of mind
That springs when it's triggered by certain keys
Then bellows like Polyphemus was blind
When he hurled huge boulders at Ulysses.
It's a bully tactic for sure, one eye
Always open, looking for trouble; then,
When poked, scrambling madly and swinging high
And low, irritated, injured again.
Those familiar learn to leave it alone;
Hand signals indicate to not go there,
But in life's soup you'll always find a bone
The bully chokes on though it's in your care.
If you want to see blind rage and raised fists
Calmly make a statement like, *God exists*.

Random House

Now that truth enrichment has been consigned
To permanent hiatus, baths of lies
To take their place on bookshelves, would you mind
Explaining how women turning to guys
And vice versa is the new world order
Such that all new publications reflect
Political correctness? The border
Crossing to what once was truth is now wrecked;
Literature now is not tradition,
The truth of the age is truth for all time,
So we can toss out every rendition
Though the end result isn't worth a dime.
When eyes have time to adjust, they will see
Emperor's new clothes forced on you and me.

In Our Hands

The purpose of life is to reveal God.
We stand before Him the best we know how
In forefather footsteps, which can seem odd
So we tweak the ways slightly but still bow
But then the point comes where bowing feels strange
Perhaps a straighter stand will do as well;
Some of these rules are restricting our range:
No one wants to hear they're going to Hell.
They want to rephrase wording of The Word.
Certain groups think it's coming on too strong;
To condemn and forgive: it's quite absurd
To have both. If God's love, then no love's wrong.
So seize the day; do anything you wish;
When God asks if we have a king, say *Fish*.

Joe-Nah!

Whale on whoever teaches right from wrong,
Whale on religion and forces for good,
Whale on order, hope chaos comes along,
Then whale on not having to knock on wood.
Hammer home your every view without shame,
Hammer them all no matter how extreme;
It's not about truth, only who's to blame,
Hammer as if you're captain of the team.
Then whale on anyone who won't agree,
Whale in public, hound them, give them no peace,
Whale them out of business, and take a knee
When told to stand for anthems and police.
Whale on truth until your mouth starts to foam,
Whale there's no God from the belly of old Rome.

A Flashing Sum of Things

Now I wait for the right rhythm and beat
To get me moving, I'll know when it hits;
Strangely enough, it brings me to my feet...
I find myself floating out of the pits.
There are strange occasional gifts it seems,
Almost magical in music and sound;
These form compelling memorable beams
Almost of light in a perfect way round.
You would know in an instant one was there,
No doubt at the outset something was new,
Rare itself, carrying all that is rare,
Part of something larger, yet a whole too.
It's like there's nothing great and nothing small:
In truth, for each part vibrates with it all.

Static

On my approach, there is so much static;
We asked for this, or did any of us?
We still got it; it was automatic
Including the impotence of a fuss.
Nothing changes no matter what we see,
But something changes us when we see straight;
Reality is and will always be
Obvious yet elusive as we wait.
Along the way, it clarifies, or turns
So hard it blocks all light from passing through.
Clarified only means that one discerns
There's more, where those who block are nothing new
It's common to deny what one can't hold
Soon we're all covered with lines where we fold.

City Crossing

I'm like the city night, with its bums and whores
Dilapidated liquor stores, its lights,
Gangs on corners racking up their scores
Especially Chicago city nights—
By Humboldt Park street-wise dogs cross streets
Light after light, similar scenes of man
Without Christ, and yet Christ's statue greets
You—offers peace to every Caliban
Church after church, north, south, east and west
It doesn't end. The whole night reeks
Of foul assortment of eggs in Satan's nest
Incubating, hatched by the slightest tweaks
Yet there it is, the hand with the central scar
Blessing me as I slouch forward in my car

Perfect Ten

What seemed special was how we threw the dart
Or made jokes, winking with a certain flair,
Points for style, but common sense is an art,
And to really have it is something rare.
It's true the world's full of relative gifts,
And there's a veil of darkness that deceives
Us into belief that flowing with shifts
Away from truth is normal: that truth leaves
One unsure what it is, all things unclear.
That's our first mistake and leads to our last,
Which is that we think of God without fear
He's real and expects us to hold steadfast.
We miss the mark with everything at stake;
A perfect Ten for Commandments we break.

In the Dark Mix

We're much more jovial in the dark mix
and a hole is open for the chaos
to probe for a good foothold as we laugh,
that so by nightfall, as the glow wears off
and we realize we did nothing but bask
in idleness, in vanity and pride,
our dark eyes go to bed in sour contrast
to all of our previous victories...
Then we wake from dreams quite enervated,
compelled to distrust, and spewing chaos
in the dark mix where bright lights bring joy,
make easy targets, so we shoot big holes
which make good footholds as we leap headlong
only to find that chaos was there first.

Where Death Has Died

I don't think as Him, but see how He thinks;
My ways are not His, but I see His ways;
I see Him reaching out to one who sinks,
While other creatures seem content to graze.
An answer to life, one that heard life call,
As it reached a point to need something more.
A something that first gives a sense of all,
And in a dark glass shows an open door
To touch this world from inside a man's heart,
And call that heart the temple of the Lord.
The greatest minds acknowledge this in art,
Though some deny the pier where boats are moored.
We come together, look up high inside
To thoughts and ways that start where death has died

Paul's Anchor

Near Malta, Paul's ship hit sand in a gale
And broke apart. No lives, just anchors lost
Which divers claim they've found. But what we fail
To see here is despite having been tossed
About on the waves, and even shipwrecked,
Paul was ever anchored and safe in Christ
These are perilous times where faith is pecked,
Picked on and eroded, ground down and sliced
Apart, threatened by winds and dark skies now,
That we're in the same boat as Paul, no worse,
It doesn't matter what happens, just how
We stay the same course. Hardship's not a curse.
When we're gone, may our anchor too be found,
Not shipwrecked souls, but grounded, safe and sound.

The Givens

The givens, self-evident truths, are gone
As what was given can't be taken
Anymore. After thousands of years, dawn
Interrupts darkness, truth is forsaken
For new age truth, as in peace, love and dope.
So take the givens out, and start over
Don't worry about God or death or hope
And the ignorant armies of *Dover
Beach*, the night in which they clashed ends right now
We no longer look at life in this way
All are equal, free, genderless; and how
Did it come to pass? It was given, say,
A gift of new givens rammed down the throat;
A given it gets an honest man's goat

The Wind Understands

The wind understands me if it has mind
It conveys the same signals I send out
But no one feels my thoughts as I do air
Mindless gusts seem to have the upper hand
There's little to use to prove otherwise
Language gets lost the higher the tower
Still, there's substance in the nothing I feel
It isn't nothing when for me it's real
In shape and symmetries and raw power
Which show slightly here after many tries
But is it substantial like time from sand
In an hourglass? Who will see just how rare
This is, made from wind and mind like a shout?
(And what is lost when a thing is defined)

Foul Skins

I keep my diseases close to my vest
Behind the bars that put me to the test
This way, they'll only eat away at me
And do no harm to anyone I see
But somehow like a giant ball of sweat
An image of me forms that I have met —
It walks out through the bars away from me
And touches even those I cannot see
The bars grow stronger, show no signs of rust
I'm shunned as someone nobody can trust
My soul diseased, has leaked away from me
Darkness arrives and leaves no light to see.
Believing we can quarantine our sins
We populate the world with our foul skins.
    6.16.15

Fuming Rose

The rose fumed, smoked and pierced me with a thorn
in expectation I would die, before
withering itself, leaving the land dead.
It stands in full bloom again before me
fresh, emanating familiar fragrance,
beckoning me: *Come near.* Such a complex,
simple thing that taught me so much about
fate, having wrung me through it. Now after
the season of no life, mere survival,
I find this flower that I dreamed of kicking
across the field should I see it again,
yet somehow I seem to take to the earth
sink to my knees and dig myself a hole
where I'm just a grub nursing on its root

Mobilization

In their day, these were ornamental gifts
To be stared at, enjoyed for what they are.
Now under siege, we must use them for war,
See them as explosive and launch them far,
Let them make shock waves while we hear the roar
Though we must wonder what causes such shifts.
Thus a golden Byzantine bird must fly
Into phoenix-like rebirth for our sake,
And the Shield of Achilles will do well
Beyond an image as people will die
Fulfilling its depictions with a lake
That details fires breaking loose from all Hell.
All imagery we hold true turned to bombs,
From ends of our minds, even unto the palms.

High Priority

The aura I had anything to say
Is gone, and I am just another scared
Spirit at the doorway of its last day,
Not even asking myself why I dared
To think I had some knowledge to offer.
Am I not like rock that gets wet in rain?
What makes us think if we fill our coffer,
We'll avoid the inevitable pain?
So I back away from caring to try
To convince you of anything I've thought;
I'd wanted to sell it, but who would buy
What's free and what all have already got?
Just remember though when it comes your turn
The other side should be your whole concern.

Pulling the Shades

They lay down the math in deep scratching scrapes
Until we go through the tables with ease,
But with metaphysics they open drapes
With the windows closed, keeping out the breeze.
The exactitude of numbers should teach
Underlying perfection, design perhaps,
And lead to wonder what is out of reach,
Where to block that off only leaves great gaps...
We're left free when it comes to taking sides
On the truth, but that window's closing, guys;
What doesn't add up subtracts and divides,
They say, so dogmatism multiplies.
I tell you all this in slight gusts of air
Like the wind blowing softly through your hair.

To the Unborn

We who are about to die salute you:
Life is just a flesh wound forging spirit
Into a sword; if that doesn't suit you
Find the frame of mind that best comes near it.
We all catch fire if one can call it that,
Though some burn too hot and others too cool
Where those who get *le juste milieu* down pat
Deserve the opportunity to rule.
But something more of mindsets must be said,
That like an egg we're born to be consumed,
Or we crack out, free from the living dead
Who burn out in frames of mind that are doomed.
What more can I hope than my words evoke
The flame of mind that sees through shell to yolk?

Always Something

Something is going to happen today
To catch my interest, take me down its path
A toilet breaks, a friend dies, or I'll lay
Around until I need a shower or bath
I'll check the garden, pick anything ripe
Listen to the radio for the news
Do my best to separate out the hype
From the lies and locate some honest views
Ideas are like pollen, the air is thick
With it, our minds provide the fertile soil
Where weeds rampage, not long before we're sick
And no longer know peace, only turmoil
So I keep waiting, something's got to give
That life must end gives me reason to live

The Towering Oak

Someday at the towering oak you stand
Each day you lived's a leaf, now they fall...
Buried in your own hourglass, the last sand
Trickling down, burying you in your wall.
Once you hoped to be like that tree, stand strong,
Gather light, be flexible, not fall down;
But got nutrients and sandy soil wrong,
Made a swamp that caused you to wallow, drown.
So the whole idea of standing strong fails
And one's whole success is falling down hard
The soul trickles leaving sandy soil trails...
Ask who isn't dealt the wallow-drown card
But there's a door hidden on the oak's side
If you find the key, you won't be denied

Red Shift

Getting further away, alone with my stars
My galaxy grown huge over the years
Alone on the road with no other cars
I come into light as a great fog clears.
What's grown to a world I've carried for years
I thought it was all inclusive, but no...
It's mostly memories, emotions, fears
A massive ship adrift, no one to row.
The passengers though real are more like ghosts
They are not conscious though they seem alert
I pedal for them all, and each one coasts
They may have died, but in me they're unhurt.
My universe, just a bubble of mind
Where I'm the only life just I can find

Standing Before a Song

I stand before a song that must be split
and stacked into a face chord to be burned
in these cold days and nights down to each sharp
and flat, the staffs dismantled to last notes.
Now it resonates in a singular
and perfect performance, which is its will
to survive, lifting my soul to set down
the axe and listen, on one foot and then
the other, blowing heat into my hands
while my family, frigid in the house,
scrapes frosted breath from windows, peering out,
aghast I take such risks and don't comply,
dance rather than chop, stack and end the song.
Later they'll thaw as I hum it to them.

163

Phoenix

When I was a boy they warned me the fire
Would try to lure me with a subtle lie
That to speak against it made one a liar
And flames would renew me, I wouldn't die.
For years I never stoked or fanned the coals
But watched friends fly to embers in the air;
When I realized I'd never reach my goals
I played with fire because I didn't care,
I wore it like armor and felt immune.
When friends told me I'd changed, I felt betrayed
And kissed them all off into a spittoon,
Embracing my fiery self, newly made.
Years later I understood I'd been burned,
Sparks flew up, but my soul never returned.

Mountainous Betrayal

The children did not know their parents' fears,
Innocently caught in the larger plan
To appease the gods that control the spheres:
A better world from a shortened lifespan.
We, too, tie down our kids as on the mules,
Then take them up the mountain as it were,
Make them an example of how we're fools,
Pay with their souls to make ourselves secure.
See how they color their hair in rainbow,
Boys and girls believing there's no gender;
It's us pulling the strings, but they don't know,
We turned Godless and made them surrender.
By not teaching truth, we've fallen away
To sacrificing children we betray.

Room for the Devil

Outer space is like a man with no job,
Unable to do more except expand
Countless stars, his thoughts like corn off its cob
Popping up all over, not in demand.
The simple truth: focus keeps us in line;
The black hole has presence, purpose out there.
In the end, all things in the grand design
Lose momentum and join the great nowhere.
It's all streaming to center way up high,
We can't see it, but know it anyway.
The same goes for us, no need to ask why;
We just do our job and collect our pay.
When space is empty but for one black hole
Its job will be to hold an empty soul

Forensic Waffle

Floating out of aftermath I soon reached
A new beginning in what looked like scarred
No Man's Land, by chlorine gas burned and bleached,
Feathers already gone before they tarred;
But life starts over, near trenches in France,
Grass softens the huge artillery holes
Above deep caves where men chiseled romance
In stone by candlelight below blown bowls,
Mortared rain and blood, pestled lead and bone,
Poured over in a great explosive heave
On such a scale that no one can atone;
Dark underside of what man can achieve.
So take heart, what comes is just new quagmire
Think of caves you'll light with your candle fire.

The Candidate

Something he didn't see before the shell
Got him was everywhere under his nose
But the gravel roads didn't ring a bell
And he only half saw when in a pose
Which was all the time on the campaign trail
He came to the mountains to get our vote
Promised if elected he wouldn't fail
To remember us, then out on his boat
The next week, he didn't notice the oil
On the dock, nor cigarette butts, nor sand
Everywhere. A snake started to uncoil
Indigenous, inherent in the land.
As his limo bounded through dust and grime,
He never saw the world was sick in time.

Shades of the Past

A silhouette though a window, a lamp,
Reminds me of a childhood that was lost
Shadows on screen with a familiar stamp
That I know well, down to the final cost.
That's the appearance of the distant past,
A vaguely cast yet clearly outlined view,
No real presence here and now but a vast
Occupation of my space, ghost and boo
Able any time to pop in the stream
Of consciousness, randomly to be part
Of the foreground or background like a dream,
Even to suggest meaning as in art.
Their shadows rise from swirling mists on a lake,
Where shed skins waft with the look of a snake

Making the Leap

Through all the clutter in my mind, a voice
Says, *Make the leap.* I wonder what it means
When I see no such place to make such choice,
No abyss, no overhang in nearby scenes.
As for somewhere within to make a leap,
That seems more likely as the spirit soars.
My problem has been to prefer the deep,
Below to sky above, but both have doors.
As far as jumping down inside, explore
The depths, I tend to think I know what's there
I've done that, almost lost myself before
And managed to escape by just a hair.
I'm open for an invite from the sky,
Perhaps I've held back, thinking I must fly.

Unholy Mess

Cooking to shut the opposition down:
Add salt, stir, act occupied as it fries,
Then wave them from your kitchen with a frown;
Never let them close to assail your lies,
Ignore them with a taste of a hot spoon:
Fan at your mouth to drive away the heat,
Pronounce it wonderful and ready soon,
Then serve your people, call them in to eat.
In eating there's a way of fighting back:
Blink to get a secret message across
Or sprinkle salt, write code the cook can't crack
And blow it away while passing the sauce.
Then fill pockets with vegetables and fruit,
Run the cook off and take over to boot.

An Open Mind

Just please, have an open mind, that this world
Which you find here, when born, in its present state,
That whatever the ultimate truth is,
It was here when you arrived, that's the case.
So it really doesn't need your advice;
It's not going to change on your say so.
You have to start open and take what comes,
Look in all corners of life and your heart.
Meanwhile the world has decided for you:
It says it knows and will teach you in school.
Around the world this varies as a rule,
But the answer comes first, not the question.
Just step back and review all history
Was anyone harmed by the mystery?

Futile Thought

As soon as I finish painting the shed,
I'll work on that thought I wish to express
To my friends, I hope, before they're all dead;
Cogent inside, but on paper a mess...
The shed is done, but I must mow the lawn,
Where I have so many thoughts I should write
That I can't keep track of all that I spawn
But work in ecstatic sweat and delight.
The years go by, and I've let the shed go;
The paint's peeling, but I don't really care.
My neglected lawn is too deep to mow;
The death of my friends left me in despair,
But helped that furtive thought come very clear:
It's on a sheet of paper somewhere here.

Area Fifty-Two

The winds blow over me now like a rock
As what would ripple has solidified
And receives the sounds of spirit as squawk
Over a vast dust bed where once I cried
I'm the one who numbed myself with stiff drink
Refused the tender warmth of woman's love
I decided young what takes years to think
Denying what's inside and all above
My domain stretches beyond what I see
Where I exist alone unto myself
Area Fifty-One's got zilch on me
An alien evolved from Santa's elf.
My tide of joy dried up, just fossils here
No trespassing, with good reason to fear

Celestial Mechanics

Moving out of phase from the alignment,
My lenses haze where objects that don't fade
Continue on paths without confinement,
While I deliquesce in increasing shade.
As it cools, it's like being in thick soup
Where all things mix, become one with the spice,
I'll finish my own length of the great loop
As the one part that knows, pays the price.
Whatever it was I saw as I toured
Mostly a rehash of everything seen
I tried to isolate what is obscured
By what we spew though it remains pristine
Strangely, its course is so aligned to ours
We follow it, sensing inherent powers

Relay

Here's the handoff of the world to your age
Our dusty shelf retired for yours that gleams
So many obsolete relics, our stage
Now a warehouse of props useful for memes
Something to ridicule, demean, distort
Even to deny some events occurred
The rewriting of history's a sport:
No value in truth, no keeping one's word.
Your own shelf will grow to be full one day
And all the focus will be on what's new;
Your own great moments will soon go away
To the same warehouse, nothing you can do
But flip the hourglass and pass the world on,
The shifting sands are a kind of baton.

Renaissance Unfair

What do we have to work with that has truth?
Not much overall in the great grand scheme;
All would fit in a Renaissance Fair booth
But it's better left spread out, it would seem.
There's precious little after centuries
And much was lost one way or another
The world might turn septic, but no worries:
Even if left in hands of *Big Brother,*
A coming age will somehow get it back
Through war or through a renaissance of arts...
Awake to truth when it's under attack
Then fighting to restore justice in hearts.
You'd think truth would be cherished since it's rare
But to take that booth out, they'd burn the fair.

Wrecking Song

Her song was one I never learned by heart
There are screechings and strange notes I forget
She varied her warblings into an art
And made me feel that we had never met
So I'd show up there and lurk in the hope
She'd notice me sometime during her song
I had this dream that sometime we'd elope
That I was right for her, the others wrong
As she sang I felt it was just for me
The others seemed to disappear, and though
I said nothing, I felt that she could see
What was in my heart, but it wasn't so
It was strictly for hypnotic effect
Those screechings, like mine, came from those she wrecked

Bottling Lethe

Wait until they forget, give it some years
Fifty to eighty should do, then our views
Will be new to the youth; without old fears,
And reason to question us with fresh news;
We'll seduce them like a Venus Flytrap
With fragrant promises of all that's good
Rights to work, things equal across the map
Then let them pull down articles that stood
For centuries against this very thing,
Gone in seconds what took lifetimes to grow;
Replace liberty and freedom to sing
Revolution's glory to an Uncle Joe,
Then wait in line for bread afraid to speak
And inherit winds bequeathed to the meek.

171

Inherent Dynamic

We seem made independent to transpire
Freely and without any inner need
To rely on forces that are higher,
But it's a paradox that once we're freed
From any ties to faith we start to flail
As a deficiency in spirit forms,
Hard to detect on a national scale,
With all natural divergence from norms;
But in the single heart, it's far more clear:
One benefits from belief, faith there's more,
That nothing after death brings only fear,
A sense of meaninglessness to our door.
But the inborn drive to know truth ensures
The quest to find the Holy Grail endures.

Parasitic Onslaught

Disproving the miracle from within
How is that accomplished? You make it seem
A natural fact, and then you begin
To plant notions that the truth is a dream.
Let them harangue a while. When the smoke clears
Some will side with you, claim you have merit.
Let them go to work giving birth to fears;
It won't be long before you inherit
A new generation born to follow,
Your theories now the core of their textbook.
That is the process to render hollow
A vein of its life's blood. In the next look
The mainstream will ban those old truths once taught,
Then flow free in parasitic onslaught.

Suggestion Box

In the great hall of *No one gives a crap*
There are portraits of the Hall of Famers
It shows no disrespect to take a nap
It's hoped all visitors will be shamers
So bring your *Silly String* and spray at will
Vandalize the place any way you like
Then please turn when you've had your fill
And see the grounds where you can take a hike
The statues outside are also fair game
Bags of rotten fruit to throw are for sale
The rules are let them have it, so, the same.
Give it to them by the bucket or pail
Then leave us tales of those you loath and know
And help make this awful hating place grow

Straight Jacket

You reach that terror, find the thing that will
kill you and diminish quickly to just
A straight jacket of your former self and
disappear, leaving the shirt to drop not
in fluff and air but wet and cold. The news
spreads like blood through the system reaching out
and touching to the degree that you were
partially known, where the spread is like a
life's blood to the living who see things right
for a time as after a decent meal.
From the ground, the straight jacket floating down
seems on a mission, coming straight at you.
Perhaps this is where it gets its name, and
binds you so tight you don't know what hit you.

In the Shaker

Vibrant city to ruins, to flatness and desert
As holes form underneath and suck it dry
Much as an hourglass where all turns to dirt
And drains as the clock chimes the end is nigh
At a standstill, we're in the shaker, shook
To where we're all just quickly broken down
We received a ticket with time that took
No time at all, which was told in the book,
Which we didn't read when we had the chance
For some reason we didn't care to hear,
Like down deep we knew there was just one dance
Which we sat out on and now shed a tear
Then through a blur we dance up such a storm
Our world starts breaking, sinking without form

The Sand Man

The sand man tried serving his food for years
He mixes sand with everything he makes
People always passed him by, laughed to tears
That someone would add sand to what he bakes
But strangely, he started having success
Customers began lining up outside
After trying it, they had to confess
They enjoyed it, they said. I thought they lied
I watched through the window one afternoon
They didn't chew but swallowed right away
They called it delicious, perhaps too soon
Give it some time, I figured, and they'd pay
But now the sand man decides what we eat
Through sleepless nights, we line up hungry, beat.

A Poem is More Than a Pixel

A poem is more than a pixel, it's a way
Into a mindset, making it more a hologram
An ordered flow that dips into understanding
A starting quip that teleports into an ideal.
On the edge of such vistas, the mind reacts
Like iron filings on paper covering a magnet;
From a pile of powder to overhanging ferns
Crystalline in attraction that pulls a thought
Into its own symmetries that mirror orders
Fathomed intuitively on reception, where
They take not just hold but root, not weeds
But flowers of light that dot skies at night
Over a lifetime, a new perspective's reached
Not worldly dots but features of God's face

Not So Petty Coats

When this too passes as they say it shall
Will cities be laid low in ruins again?
Will bombs be dropped to prove one's rationale
In saying something like women are men
If they only think they are, and boys girls
And can then join the women's boxing team
Then beat them so bad it straightens their curls
And win a medal for the new regime
Traditions we stood for are demonized
Legacies assaulted, and history
Distorted, everything Godly despised
How holocausts come is no mystery
People will have to fight or die like sheep
Evil's a wolf dressed like Little Bo Peep

175

The Right to Choose

Humanity at the crossroads, two trains
Are coming, you can hear the horns and see
Lights flash, the gates come down. All that remains
Is choosing one on which you wish to be
There's one track on the left, one on the right
On one you pay not long after you board
Your ticket gets punched late into the night
Speeding too fast downhill to pull the cord
The other lets you decide where to go
Differing with others on board who share
Though, the larger sense of what they all know
To be old basics that are true and fair
The other train turns and is roaring back
What started as choice is under attack
   2.11.19

Demolition Day

The ancient church had a straightforward nave
And was built to stand for thousands of years;
Now it's in ruins, not much left to save...
If it fell, the nation would be in tears.
At least that's what we thought ten years ago
Now there's talk of having it all yanked down
Because it symbolizes God, and so
His enemies on earth who always frown
On any mention, anything to do
With Him, want to make sure that it's destroyed.
It's all the same whether ancient or new,
It must be eradicated, made void.
Sad to see the church come down, but its doom
More so presages a religious boom.

One Bright Candle

Is this what it means to be human? I'm
Living in a shell of silence, I tap
The walls for signs of God. I try to climb
To survey the main structures of the trap;
I see reflections, hear echoes, but know
There's something beyond that I feel inside.
It's easy to deny it since it's so
Subtle like background noise, but far and wide,
No matter where I travel, it's right there,
More than consciousness of being awake,
Less than a watchful eye, it doesn't stare;
It's more a lone bright candle on your cake.
Why does the world demand I blow it out?
It marks a rise in faith that passes doubt

Babble

Rather than make joints secure, let them slide
Over one another so they'll collapse
As well as hold shape, make it fluid, wide
As a structure, don't worry about gaps.
Rings on poles make the whole easy to pack
Let nomadic minds from bodies in tents,
Start to wander, to climb, there's no going back,
Nothing about the enterprise makes sense,
Where far-reaching truth that's far out of reach
Makes a wide-ranging target, which is strange.
It's all been shot down, what they used to teach,
As the mainstream got shot up in the range
Plans were simple, though the purpose sounds odd:
Retractable tower; dismantle God.

Feeding the Snake

It seemed right at the time to feed the snake
As by all accounts we were in control.
By all its slithering, it couldn't make
The top of its container as its goal.
By all appearances, just to escape
Was all it cared about. We didn't see
That every inch it grew was like duct tape
Around our feet first, up like a mummy
Until it had us, engulfed, constricted,
And there honestly wasn't a way out.
That's what it whispered. We were conflicted,
Started believing it without a doubt.
Now we know we should have stepped on its head
When we found it, not nurture it instead.

Navigating the Flood

Words arranged by clear thought straighten the mind
As close as one can come to thought that's pure
That recognizes every other kind
And chooses not diseases but the cure
The heart knows where to find this well to drink
It knows as soon as hears if it's on track
But the world's a mix of the few who think
At peace, and those who can't on the attack
Nice to be spirit and not have to breathe
But mind depends on flesh and bones and blood
It's a constantly surging moil and seethe;
You must navigate through a turgid flood
Of minds choking; everyone has a beef
Just put it out there: the truth spells relief

Guidance from Night

After years of gradual shifting gears
Away from a moral center to what
Seems right based on shallow Godless fears
Ideas that by logic can't make the cut
People no longer think; they only feel
Their way along where truth is the last thing
They care about; they think it isn't real
But the ends they want, anything to bring
Those home is in the toolbox, violence, lies
There's no evil if in the end what's good
As you see it comes, no matter who dies
Pinocchio here wants to turn to wood
The world seems to prefer guidance from night
Going the speed of indifference to light

Infant in the Making

Please come look at the perfect sleeping child,
Which for a moment has settled in peace;
You look, and something in you's reconciled,
In just a moment, the wonder will cease.
Imagine making this yourself from scratch,
Testing looks before turning on power,
You might have tried an egg and let it hatch
Or plant, add water and watch it flower.
But though we don't have any such control,
There's a kind of infant I'm making here:
It will adopt you and give you a soul,
It won't change, but you'll grow, just to be clear.
I send it out now, breathing on its own
If it wakes you up, you'll see how you've grown

179

Cry of the Om Mighty

The OMMM of the Zen master has a vibe
That resonates as if to shatter glass
The waves too pound home that you're in the tribe
Of natives converted who attend Mass
Life seems pulled across like a circus tent
And we're all underneath watching the show
Acts of danger, where acrobats who meant
To stay safely high are shot down, brought low
I pound the drum to summon all good hearts
But the ringmaster competes with his mic
Stars on the canvas hide where the tent starts
The Dutch boy lost his finger in this dike
The circus bosses want him put to sleep
A shattering OMMM cries out from the deep

Maze of Contradictions

Teaching of morality without God
Has come to be the norm. That they borrow
The same precepts minus faith might seem odd,
But it doesn't help the greater sorrow.
Kant made the moral imperatives clear,
Which went to actions, axioms of will,
To what is universal and what's near.
But why isn't God one thou shalt not kill?
Without Him, blind, we still search for His ways,
Which we find inside, prove what we deny...
He made it simple. Ten laws, not this maze
Of contradictions we get around them by.
Someday our age will be seen for all its lies:
Manure to suffocate, not fertilize.

Sabotage

We are on an ocean, swirling our way
In the vast darkness of an endless space,
Fighting with one another night and day
Like hamsters on their wheels, running a race
The ozone hole and a plastic island
Command little attention, nor the rain
Forests disappearing, books being banned...
Hard to say the whole world isn't insane.
But as we drift at the whim of this sea
It begins to dawn on more than a few
That the issue is ideology,
Several, not a single one that's new,
With all of them vying to take control
And sabotage what makes one free and whole.

Shared Hope

Those bereft in hope lead you where there's none
But as the nature of things tends to fray
Within the swamp tank, who can say he's won
When soon enough fullness turns to decay
The triumphs are recorded though in works
From masters of the past who left their mark
Graffiti too shows there were even jerks
In Pompeii before days the sky turned dark
Some of my friends are gone, others bemoan
Their lot, look upon family and friends
As rotting, empty, hopeless, and their tone
Is: lack of meaning justifies such ends
But when they ask why don't I feel despair
The battle's won, so that is what I share

Last Traces

Making an outline of the horizon
Out my window, marking the tree line
Against the sky, with both sets of eyes on,
Those that see the physical world's design,
And those that have the vision inside
That sense transcendent spirit when it's clear,
I continue to let my finger glide.
A stained-glass window begins to appear;
I watch as the couch becomes an altar,
And the living room turns into a nave.
Pouring lead, my finger frames a psalter,
Flowing red, then I'm lifted from my grave.
Friends and family gathered by my bed
Watch my finger drop, wondering what it said.

In the End

I lose my name in service to the truth.
What glory in the end to just speak plain?
In the end, fame's just a desire of youth;
It's understanding in the end you gain.
But imagine being all knotted up
In a wrong point of view you think is right:
Sipping all those years from an empty cup,
You'd be hard to untie wound up so tight.
Thinking well and clearly is not easy.
No doctrine's worth its salt if it's not sound;
The crimes of logic should make us queasy,
But who'll admit their viewpoint has no ground?
I'm only telling you this as a friend
In the end there will be no end. The end.

Titles

185

Sonnets